THE WOMEN OF LLANRUMNEY

By / Gan Azuka Oforka

Cast

Cerys **Keziah Joseph**
Simon Taylor, Tommy Flynn and / a Mr Ainsworth **Matthew Gravelle**
Elizabeth **Nia Roberts**
Annie **Suzanne Packer**

Creative Team / Tîm Creadigol

Director / Cyfarwyddwr **Patricia Logue**
Designer / Cynllunydd **Stella-Jane Odoemelam**
Assistant Director / Cyfarwyddwr Cynorthwyol **Keish Peets**
Lighting Designer / Cynllunydd Goleuo **Andy Pike**
Composer / Cyfansoddwr **Takisha Sargent**
Sound Designer / Chynllunydd Sain **Ian Barnard**
Fight Director / Cyfarwyddwr Ymladd **Kevin McCurdy**
Wellbeing Coach / Hyfforddwr Lles **Ndidi John**
Dialect Coach / Hyfforddwr Tafodiaith **Rhian Cronshaw**
Rehearsal and production photographer / Ffotograffydd Ymarfer a Chynhyrchiad **Ana Pinto**
BSL interpreter / Dehonglydd BSL **Nikki Champagnie Harris**
Audio Describer / Sain Ddisgrifydd **Michelle Perez**
Captioner / Capsiwnwr **Erika James**

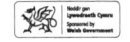

Sherman Cymru Productions Ltd | Registered Charity Number / Rhif Elusen Cofrestredig 1118364

Production Team / Tîm Cynhyrchu

Production Manager / Rheolwr Cynhyrchu
Mandy Ivory-Castile

Company Stage Manager / Rheolwr Llwyfan y Cwmni
Josh Miles

Deputy Stage Manager / Dirprwy Reolwr Llwyfan
Theodore Hung

Assistant Stage Manager / Rheolwr Llwyfan Cynorthwyol
Enfys Clara

Technical Manager / Rheolwr Technegol
Rachel Mortimer

Technicians / Technegwyr
Olwen Barnes-Archer, Emily Howard, Ruby James

RWCMD Student Technical Theatre Placement
Lleoliad Theatr Dechnegol Myfyrwyr CBCDC
Aneurin Whelan

Workshop Manager / Rheolwr Gweithdy
Alasdair Head

Construction / Adeiladwaith
Mathew Thomas, Will Hawkins, Stanley Walling

Scenic Artists / Artistiaid Golygfaol
Vada Baldwin, Emily Jones, Maisie Wolstenholme

Costume Supervisor / Goruchwyliwr Gwisgoedd
Fenna de Jonge

Costume Assistants / Cynorthwywyr Gwisgoedd
Celia Favorite, Buddug Hickson-Langford, Nikita Verboon

Thanks / Diolch
Llanrumney Hall
Hasia Akwaboah, Malcom Bishop, Karen Kisakye, Cassius Konneh, Tumba Katanda
Siân McCabe at Welsh National Opera / yn Opera Cenedlaethol Cymru

The Women of Llanrumney was first performed on 16 May 2024.
Perfformiwyd *The Women of Llanrumney* am y tro cyntaf ar 16 Mai 2024.

MAKING THEATRE IS A TEAM EFFORT. IT REQUIRES A BROAD RANGE OF SKILLS AND EXPERTISE TO MAKE A PRODUCTION HAPPEN. THIS IS THE SHERMAN TEAM: / GWAITH TÎM YW CREU THEATR. MAE GOFYN AM YSTOD EANG O SGILIAU AC ARBENIGEDD I GREU CYNHYRCHIAD. DYMA DÎM Y SHERMAN:

Executive / Gweithredol

Artistic Director / Cyfarwyddwr Artistig
Joe Murphy

Chief Executive / Prif Weithredwr
Julia Barry

Artistic Administration / Gweinyddiaeth Artistig

Producing and Programming Manager
Rheolwr Cynhyrchu a Rhaglennu
Patricia O'Sullivan

Creative Engagement / Ymgysylltu Creadigol

Creative Engagement Manager
Rheolwr Ymgysylltu Creadigol
Francesca Pickard

Creative Engagement Assistant
Cynorthwyydd Ymgysylltu Creadigol
Ffion Denman

Finance and Administration / Cyllid a Gweinyddiaeth

Head of Finance and Administration
Pennaeth Cyllid a Gweinyddiaeth
Sally Shepherd

Company Administrator / Gweinyddwr Cwmni
Helen Macintyre

Finance and Administration Assistant
Cynorthwyydd Cyllid a Gweinyddiaeth
Mikey Porter

Front of House / Blaen y Tŷ

Head of Operations / Pennaeth Gweithrediadau
Kevin Burt

Visitor Experience and Volunteers Manager
Rheolwr Profiad Ymwelwyr a Gwirfoddolwyr
Aled Wyn Thomas

Bar and Kitchen Manager / Rheolwr y Bar a'r Gegin
Anne Marie Saunders

Bar and Kitchen Supervisor / Goruchwyliwr y Bar a'r Gegin
Elicia Axon

Bar and Kitchen Assistants / Cynorthwywyr Bar a Chegin
Nimat Awoyemi, Tom Bentley, Katie Dobbins, Joel Edwards, Cata Lindegaard, Macsen McKay, Maddie Miles, Roisin Miller-O'Brien, Scarlett Morley, Ben Moruzzi, Alexander Prime, Gethin Roberts

Fundraising and Development / Codi Arian a Datblygu

Head of Fundraising and Development
Pennaeth Codi Arian a Datblygu
Emma Tropman

Literary / Llenyddol

Literary Manager / Rheolwr Llenyddol
Davina Moss

Literary Associate / Cydymaith Llenyddol
Lowri Morgan

Marketing and Communications / Marchnata a Chyfathrebu

Head of Marketing and Communications
Pennaeth Marchnata a Chyfathrebu
Ed Newsome

Marketing Manager / Rheolwr Marchnata
Alice Smith

Press Manager (Freelance) / Rheolwr y Wasg (Llawrydd)
Catrin Rogers

Box Office Supervisors / Goruchwylwyr y Swyddfa Docynnau
Scott Frankton, Llion Parry

Box Office Assistants / Cynorthwywyr y Swyddfa Docynnau
Owen Alun, Charla Grace, Johnny Harman, Alice Kilgarriff, Eileen Leahy, Lowri Morgan, Elizabeth Ribchester, Gethin Roberts

Production and Planning / Cynhyrchu a Chynllunio
Head of Production and Planning
Pennaeth Cynhyrchu a Chynllunio
Mandy Ivory-Castile

Company Stage Manager / Rheolwr Llwyfan y Cwmni
Josh Miles

Technical Manager / Rheolwr Technegol
Rachel Mortimer

Workshop Manager / Rheolwr Gweithdy
Alasdair Head

Thank you to our incredible Volunteer Ushers:
Diolch yn fawr i'n Tywyswyr Gwirfoddol anhygoel:
Abbas Radaideh, Ali Robinson, Alyssa Aziz, Amy Woods, Anna Lam, Ben Ping, Cate Welsh, Charles Gabe, Chloe Parkes, Claire Anderson, Clive Rudge, Clive Ward, Dana Tait, Dave Webb, David Jones, David Prew, Dylan Chichester, Eileen Leahy, Emily Allan, Germaine Walsh, Grace Uruski, Hannah Quinn, Helen Rankmore, India Thomas, Irina Guliaeva, Jenny Cripps, Jen Sutton, Kalila Bradley, Katie Brown, Kevin Chubb, Leah Kerr, Lizzie Moreland, Lucia Taher, Lucinda Devine, Madalena Juma, Magdalena Sowka, Martin Gray, Mary Prew, Mary Rudge, Martin Gray, Matthew Bedford, Mehdi Razi, Nick Fisk, Paige Cooper, Paul Mitchell, Peter Gaskell, Radu Harnu, Rhys Evans, Rubie Fallon, Sean Parker, Sian Davies, Sue Hayes, Taskin Ar-Rafee, Terri Delahunty, Theo Greenwood, Tom Rhys, Tony Wu, Zeljka Whittaker

BOARD OF TRUSTEES / YMDDIRIEDOLWYR
Ceri Davies *(Chair / Cadeirydd)*
Rhian Head *(Vice Chair / Is-gadeirydd)*
Nicholas Carlton
Llinos Daniel
Alex Hicks
Ifty Khan
David King MBE
Márta Minier
Gary Owen
Marc Simcox
Huw Thomas
Louise Thomas
Owen Thomas
Jane Tyler
Helen Vallis

WELCOME / CROESO

Welcome to *The Women of Llanrumney*, whether you are joining us in person or are reading at home. We are so thrilled to be able to share Azuka Oforka's extraordinary new play with you.

Croeso i *The Women of Llanrumney*, p'un a ydych yn ymuno â ni yn y theatr neu'n darllen adref. Rydym mor falch o rannu drama newydd a rhyfeddol Azuka Oforka gyda chi.

Joe Murphy
Artistic Director
Cyfarwyddwr Artistig

Julia Barry
Chief Executive
Prif Weithredwr

NOTES FROM THE WRITER
NODIADAU GAN YR YSGRIFENNWR

During the Atlantic Slave Trade, an estimated 12 million Africans were kidnapped and sold into slavery. An estimated 2 million of these captives lost their lives at sea and were thrown overboard. Millions more were born into chattel slavery and forced to work in torturous conditions in agricultural prison camps, known as plantations. Generation after generation for hundreds of years. Despite this brutal oppression and relentless dehumanisation enslaved people resisted subjugation at every turn, through resistance and rebellion they were in a constant war to assert their humanity, and this is the theme at the heart of the play.

Yn ystod Masnach Gaethweision yr Iwerydd, amcangyfrifwyd bod 12 miliwn o Affricanwyr wedi'u herwgipio a'u gwerthu i gaethwasiaeth. Amcangyfrifir bod 2 filiwn o'r carcharorion hyn wedi colli eu bywydau ar y môr cyn cael eu taflu i'r dŵr. Ganed miliynau yn rhagor i gaethwasiaeth siátel a'u gorfodi i weithio dan amodau arteithiol mewn gwersylloedd carcharorion amaethyddol, a elwir yn blanhigfeydd. Cenhedlaeth ar ôl cenhedlaeth am gannoedd o flynyddoedd. Er gwaetha'r gormes creulon hwn a'r dad-ddyneiddio di-baid, fe barhaodd y bobl oedd wedi'u caethiwo i wrthsefyll darostyngiad dro ar ôl tro. Trwy wrthwynebiad a gwrthryfel, roeddent mewn rhyfel cyson i fynnu eu dynoliaeth, a dyma'r thema sydd wrth wraidd y ddrama.

Azuka Oforka
Writer / Ysgrifennwr

SHERMAN
THEATR•THEATRE

CARDIFF'S THEATRE FOR WALES

Imagine a world made more equitable, more compassionate, more unified by the power of theatre. We are driven to achieve this vision every day. We do this by creating and curating shared live theatre experiences that inspire people from all backgrounds across South Wales to make a better world, in their own way. We believe that access to creativity and self-expression is a right and we constantly strive to ensure everyone has the opportunity to be enriched by the art of theatre.

THEATR I GYMRU YNG NGHAERDYDD

Dychmygwch fyd lle gall pŵer y theatr greu byd tecach, mwy tosturiol ac unedig. Cawn ein hysgogi i gyflawni'r weledigaeth yma yn ddyddiol. Rydyn ni'n gwneud hyn drwy greu a churadu profiadau theatr byw i'w rhannu ac i ysbrydoli pobl o bob cefndir ar draws De Cymru i fedru gwneud byd gwell, yn eu ffordd eu hunain. Credwn fod pawb â'r hawl i gael mynediad at greadigrwydd a hunanfynegiant, ac ymdrechwn yn gyson i sicrhau bod pawb yn cael y cyfle i gael eu cyfoethogi gan y theatr.

SHERMANTHEATRE.CO.UK

CAST

KEZIAH JOSEPH
Cerys

Theatre includes / Theatr yn cynnwys: *The Wind in the Willows* (Shakespeare North Playhouse); *Family Tree* (Brixton House Theatre & UK Tour / Taith DU); *Hot in Here* (Camden People's Theatre & UK Tour / Taith DU); *Tamed* (Norwich Theatre); *Family Tree* (Young Vic); *The Language of Kindness* (Wayward Productions / Complicité UK Tour / Taith DU); *The Lion, The Witch and The Wardrobe* (Bridge Theatre); *Mr Gum and the Dancing Bear: The Musical!* (National Theatre); *Sweeney Todd* (Liverpool Everyman); *The Paper Man* (Tobacco Factory & Soho Theatre); *Dick Whittington* (Lyric Hammersmith); *As You Like It* (Regent's Park Open Air Theatre); *The Jungle Book* (Royal & Derngate); *Kanye the First* (HighTide UK Tour / Taith DU); *Silver Lining* (Rose Theatre Kingston UK Tour / Taith DU).

Audio includes / Sain yn cynnwys: *Faith, Hope & Glory, The Mother, Assata Shakur: The FBI's Most Wanted Woman, Agnes Grey, Between Ballard's Ears, Love (sic), Love Me, The Thickness, Watership Down, Northanger Abbey, Wild Things, The Bone Orchard, Somewhere in England, The Confidential Agent, The Hatton Garden Heist, The Archers* (BBC Radio 4); *Don Juan* (BBC Radio 3); *The Magic Mountain* (Allegra Productions); *Doctor Who – Antilla The Lost, Doctor Who – Cold Vengeance* (Big Finish Productions); *Crush Hour: The Musical* (Universal & Mercury Studios).

MATTHEW GRAVELLE
Simon Taylor, Tommy Flynn and Mr Ainsworth

Theatre includes / Theatr yn cynnwys: *Look Back in Anger* (Northcott Theatre).

Television includes / Teledu yn cynnwys: *Steel Town Murders* (ITV); *The Day of the Jackal* (Amazon); *The Gold* (BBC); *Dal y Mellt* (S4C); *Carnival Row* (Amazon); *Itopia* (S4C); *The Pact* (BBC); *Silent Witness* (BBC); *Manhunt* (ITV); *The Snow Spider*

(BBC); *The Widow* (ITV); *Pluen Eira* (S4C); *Keeping Faith* (BBC Wales / S4C); *Broadchurch* (ITV); *Byw Celwydd* (S4C); *35 Diwrnod* (S4C); *Hinterland* (BBC / S4C); *Rosemary's Baby* (NBC); *Reit Tu Ôl i Ti* (S4C); *The Bible* (History Channel); *Baker Boys* (BBC); *Collision* (ITV); *Teulu* (S4C); *Pen Talar* (S4C); *Con Passionate* (S4C); *The Bench* (BBC); *Torchwood* (BBC); *Y Pris* (S4C); *Caerdydd* (S4C); *Love Soup* (BBC); *Large* (BBC); *The Scarlet Pimpernel* (BBC); *Hearts and Bones* (BBC); *Fun at the Funeral Parlour* (BBC); *Belonging* (BBC Wales); *Nuts and Bolts* (HTV Wales); *Holby City* (BBC); *Autumn Tints* (pilot) (BBC Wales).

Film includes / Ffilm yn cynnwys: *Son of God, Patagonia, Mark of Cain.*

Radio includes / Radio yn cynnwys: *The Citadel, Devoted, Curious Under The Stars, Fault Lines, How To Survive The Roman Empire* (BBC); *The Medici, Another Place, Mabinogi, Safe From Harm, Exile, Curious Under the Stars, Ten Days That Shook The World, Green Hollow, Christmas with Bryn Terfel, Ours of the Day, The Golden Record, Everyone's Got a Story, The Sum, Modesty Blaise, The Beach of Falesa, Antony & Cleopatra, The Wire, Know Your Enemy, The Icelandic Journals Headlines History, LL-Files, Sebsatian De'th, A Little Refrigerator of My Own, Mattie & Blue Bottle, The Caravan, Aberystwyth Mon Amour, The Presence* (BBC Wales); *Dead Weather / Oil on Water* (Afonica Ltd); *Bloody Eisteddfod* (Cwmni THR); *The Citadel* (BBC Audio Drama); *Francis Kilvert's Diary* (Pier Productions); *Tracks* (S4C); *The Aeneid, Red Star Newport, The Diary of Samuel Pepys, When Greed Becomes Hunger, Aberystwyth Noir, Rapid Response, Deep Country, The Gun, This Is My Mark, Torchwood, Golden Swirls, Degrees of Distance, Eyewitness* (BBC Radio 4); *Those That Can't, Last Tango in Aberystwyth, The Rocky Foundation* (BBC Radio Wales).

NIA ROBERTS
Elizabeth

For Sherman Theatre / Ar gyfer Theatr y Sherman: Titania and / a Hippolyta in / yn *A Midsummer's Night Dream, Hedda Gabler, The Get Together, Cynnau Tân*.

Theatre includes / Theatr yn cynnwys: *Blue* (Chippy Lane Productions); *Esther, Rhith Gân* (Theatr Genedlaethol Cymru); *Lovely Evening* (Young Vic); *Love Steals Us from Loneliness* (National Theatre Wales); *Stone City Blue* (Theatr Clwyd);

Ping (Music Theatre Wales); *Cymbeline; Under Milk Wood; Cider with Rosie* (Wales Theatre Company).

Television includes / Teledu yn cynnwys: Leading role Margaret in / Rôl arweiniol Margaret yn *Tree on a Hill / Pren ar y Bryn* (nominated for Best Actress at RTS Wales / enwebwyd am yr Actores Orau yn RTS Cymru) (BBC / S4C); leading role Della Howells in two seasons of / rôl arweiniol Della Howells mewn dau dymor o *Yr Amgueddfa / The Museum* (S4C / BBC iPlayer); *Steeltown Murders* (BBC); *Red Rose* (BBC / Netflix); *Hidden / Craith* (BBC / S4C); *Washington* (History Channel); *Bang* series 1 and 2 / Cyfres 1 a 2 (S4C); *The Crown* (Netflix); *Under Milk Wood* (BBC); *The White Princess* (Starz Network); *Rillington Place* (BBC); *Doctor Who* (BBC); *Hinterland* (BBC); *Keeping Faith* (BBC); *Pili Pala* (S4C); *To Provide all People, Under Milk Wood* (BBC 4); *Gifted* (Sky Arts); *Small Country, Crash, Dr Terrible's House of Horrible, Doctors, Score, Border Cafe, Outside the Rules, Collision, Hotel Babylon, Holby City, Sunburn, Casualty, Dirty Work, The Bill, Midsommer Murders, Tattoo You* (BBC); *In the Company of Strangers* (ITV – BAFTA nomination / Enwebiad BAFTA); *35 Diwrnod, Pen Talar, Y Pris, Y Palmant Aur, Fondu, Rhyw a Deinasors, Teulu, Pianissimo, Sion a Sian, Dal Yma Nawr* (S4C).

Film includes / Ffilm yn cynnwys: *The Feast / Gwledd, Last Summer, Just Jim, Under Milk Wood, Bridgend, Patagonia, Snowcake, Third Star, The Facility,* Gaenor in Oscar-nominated *Solomon a Gaenor* (BAFTA nomination); *Lois* (BAFTA win).

Radio includes / Radio yn cynnwys: *Ci Du* (Radio Cymru); *Found, Castle of the Hawk, Cymbeline, Missing Olga* (Radio 4); *Hogia'r Band of Hope, Shakespeare and Me, The Heaven Tree, Those That Can't* (Radio Wales).

SUZANNE PACKER
Annie

Suzanne Packer is a Sherman Theatre Associate Artist.

Mae Sauzanne Packer yn Artist Cyswllt Theatr y Sherman.

For Sherman Theatre / Ar gyfer Theatr y Sherman: *A Hero of The People, A Blow to Bute Street.*

Theatre includes / Theatr yn cynnwys: *Tiger Bay – The Musical, Henry VI* (Wales Millennium Centre / Canolfan Mileniwm Cymru); *A Midsummer Night's Dream* (US Tour / Taith UDA); *Up Against the Wall* (Black Co-op

Theatre); *The Crucible* (Touring Consortium); *Measure for Measure* (Aquila Theatre Co US Tour / Taith UDA); *Once on This Island*, *The Threepenny Opera* (Birmingham Repertory Theatre); *Romeo & Juliet*, *Yerma* (Bristol Old Vic); *On A Level* (Stratford East); *Our Country's Good* (English Stage Company & Tour / Taith); *Carmen Jones*, *Lady Be Good* (Crucible Sheffield); *Porgy & Bess* (Glyndebourne); *The Recruiting Officer*, *A Hero's Welcome* (Royal Court); *A Midsummer Night's Dream* (Library Theatre Manchester); *Sweet Lorraine* (Old Fire Station Oxford); *Weathering the Storm* (West Yorkshire Playhouse); *Seeing the Light* (Belfast); *Little Shop of Horrors* (Leeds Playhouse); *Dreams With Teeth*, *Power Of Darkness*, *Playboy of the West Indies*, *To Kill a Mockingbird* (Contact Theatre Manchester).

Television includes / Teledu yn cynnwys: *Tree on a Hill* (S4C / BBC Wales); *The Bay* (ITV); *Black Cab* (RS Film Productions); *Silent Witness* (BBC); *Midsomer Murders* (ITV); *Ridley* (ITV); *Agatha Raisin* (Sky / Acorn TV); *Cyswllt* (Vox Pictures / S4C); *The Pembrokeshire Murders* (ITV); *McDonald & Dodds* (ITV); *In My Skin* – Series 1 and 2 / Cyfres 1 a 2 (BBC); *Clink* (5Star); *Keeping Faith* (BBC), *Hold The Sunset* – Series / Cyfres 2 (BBC); *The ABC Murders* (BBC); *Doctor Who* (BBC); *To Provide All People* (BBC); *God Save the Kings* (TV Globo); *Bang* (S4C); *Death in Paradise* (BBC); *Edith* (BBC); *Vera* (ITV); *The Level* (ITV); *Stella* (Sky); *Doctors* (BBC); *Casualty* (BBC); *High Hopes* (BBC); *The Really Welsh Christmas Show* (BBC Wales); *Celebrity Love 4 Language* (S4C); *Dirty Works* (BBC); *Brothers and Sisters* (BBC); *Tiger Bay* (BBC Wales); *Porkpie* (Channel 4); *Grange Hill* (BBC); *Strangers in the Night* (BBC); *Some Kind of Life* (ITV); *Lifeboat* (Bloom Street); *All Good Friends* (ITV); *Brookside* (Channel 4).

Film includes / Ffilm yn cynnwys: *Warchief*.

Radio includes / Radio yn cynnwys: *Broken Colours, BBC Wales Afternoon Show, We Are Family, Sunday Morning with Colin and Suzanne, Dangerous Visions: Freedom* (BBC Radio 4); *Tracks, Jailbird Lover* (BBC Radio).

Voiceover includes / Trosleisio yn cynnwys: *The Pembrokeshire Murders, The Richest Man in the World, Coal Exchange, They Sold a Million – Shirley Bassey.*

CREATIVE TEAM / TÎM CREADIGOL

AZUKA OFORKA
Writer / Ysgrifennwr

Azuka Oforka is a playwright and screenwriter, born and raised in London, who relocated to Cardiff in 2012.

Experience includes Sherman Theatre's Unheard Voices, Critical Mass Writers Group and Invited Writers Group (Royal Court Theatre), R&D commission from The Other Room Theatre for *The Last Bastion*, BBC Writersroom Drama Room 2021 shortlist, and BBC Writersroom Welsh Voices 2022, BBC Studios / Thousand Films Thousand Stories longlist.

She is a participant in the inaugural Jed Mercurio Mentorship Programme, where she is developing an original TV pilot under the mentorship of writer and showrunner Emma Frost. She is also a participant on the ScreenSkills Regional Breakthrough Writers programme developing an original tv drama with 5Acts productions. She is passionate about telling stories that centre flawed, complex women and shine a light on underrepresented, marginalised communities in both contemporary and historical settings.

Mae Azuka Oforka yn ddramodydd ac ysgrifennwr i'r sgrin. Wedi'i geni a'i magu yn Llundain, symudodd i Gaerdydd yn 2012.

Mae ei phrofiad yn cynnwys rhaglen Unheard Voices Theatr y Sherman, Critical Mass Writers Group ac Invited Writers Group (Royal Court Theatre), comisiwn ymchwil a datblygu ar gyfer *The Last Bastion* gan The Other Room Theatre, rhestr fer BBC Writersroom Drama Room 2021, a BBC Writersroom Welsh Voices 2022, rhestr hir BBC Studios / Thousand Films Thousand Stories.

Mae hi'n rhan o Raglen Fentora gyntaf Jed Mercurio, lle bydd yn datblygu peilot gwreiddiol i'r teledu o dan fentoriaeth yr ysgrifennwr a'r rhedwr sioe Emma Frost. Mae hi hefyd yn gyfranogwr ar raglen Breakthrough Writers Rhanbarthol ScreenSkills yn datblygu drama deledu wreiddiol gyda chynyrchiadau 5Acts. Teimlai'n angerddol dros adrodd straeon sy'n canolbwyntio ar fenywod cymhleth ac yn rhoi sylw i gymunedau ymylol sydd wedi'u tangynrychioli mewn lleoliadau cyfoes a hanesyddol.

PATRICIA LOGUE
Director / Cyfarwyddwr

Patricia Logue is a Sherman Theatre Associate Artist.

For Sherman Theatre as a director: *Lose Yourself*.

She also produced and directed Beckett's *NOT I* which featured in the Sherman's Autumn 2016 Season. Patricia has also worked across multiple Sherman productions as a dialect specialist.

She is a senior acting tutor and director at the Royal Welsh College of Music & Drama and directing credits there include *Playhouse Creatures, Top Girls, Sweat, The Moors, Stupid F**king Bird, The Vibrator Play, Therese Raquin* and numerous Shakespeare productions. Patricia has worked extensively in theatre, tv and film as a dialect specialist. Her most recent credits include *Faith Healer* at Lyric Hammersmith, and NYE; *Dancing at Lughnasa* and *Romeo & Julie* for the National Theatre (co-production with Sherman Theatre).

Mae Patricia Logue yn Artist Cyswllt Theatr y Sherman.

Ar gyfer Theatr y Sherman fel cyfarwyddwr: *Lose Yourself*.

Fe wnaeth hi hefyd gynhyrchu a chyfarwyddo *NOT I* gan Beckett a ymddangosodd yn Nhymor yr Hydref 2016 y Sherman. Mae Patricia hefyd wedi gweithio ar draws nifer o gynyrchiadau'r Sherman fel arbenigwraig tafodiaith.

Mae hi'n uwch diwtor actio a chyfarwyddwr yng Ngholeg Brenhinol Cerdd a Drama Cymru ac yno, mae ei chredydau cyfarwyddo yn cynnwys *Playhouse Creatures, Top Girls,* Sweat, *The Moors, Stupid F**king Bird, The Vibrator Play, Therese Raquin* a nifer o gynyrchiadau Shakespeare. Mae Patricia wedi gweithio'n eang ym myd theatr, teledu a ffilm fel arbenigwraig tafodieithol. Mae ei chredydau diweddaraf yn cynnwys *Faith Healer* yn Lyric Hammersmith, a NYE; *Dancing at Lughnasa* a *Romeo & Julie* ar gyfer y National Theatre (cyd-gynhyrchiad gyda Theatr y Sherman).

STELLA-JANE ODOEMELAM
Designer / Cynllunydd

Stella-Jane Odoemelam is a theatre designer and practitioner, specialising in the professional construction of costume and set within her work. Her background ranges across theatre, film, live events and performance design. From a young age and throughout her career she has been immersed in live events and theatre and has established a concrete, ethical and sustainable consciousness to her work. Her work often takes on a playful and imaginative form, exploring various abstract and distinct ways of storytelling, from audience interaction, to creating immersive experiences through design, working collaboratively with a diverse range of backstage teams, touring and executing leading events, to teaching and delivering practical workshops and short courses on design, theatre and making for stage and performance.

Mae Stella-Jane Odoemelam yn gynllunydd ac ymarferydd theatr, sy'n arbenigo mewn adeiladwaith proffesiynol set a gwisgoedd o fewn ei gwaith. Mae ei chefndir yn amrywio ar draws theatr, ffilm, digwyddiadau byw a llunio perfformiadau. Ers yn ifanc a thrwy gydol ei gyrfa mae hi wedi ymgolli mewn digwyddiadau byw a theatr ac wedi sefydlu ymwybyddiaeth gadarn, foesegol a chynaliadwy yn ei gwaith. Mae ei gwaith yn aml ar ffurf chwareus a dychmygus, gan archwilio ffyrdd haniaethol ac unigryw o adrodd straeon, o ryngweithio â'r gynulleidfa, i greu profiadau trochi trwy chynllunio, cydweithio ag ystod amrywiol o dimau cefn llwyfan, cynnal a mynd â digwyddiadau blaenllaw ar daith, i addysgu a darparu gweithdai ymarferol a chyrsiau byr ar gynllunio, theatr a chreu ar gyfer llwyfan a pherfformiad.

KEISH PEETS
Assistant Director / Cyfarwyddwr Cynorthwyol

Theatre includes / Theatr yn cynnwys: As Technical Theatre Apprentice at Wales Millennium Centre / Fel Prentis Theatr Dechnegol yng Nghanolfan Mileniwm Cymru: *La Cenerentola, Roberto Devereux* (WNO), *Wicked, Matilda the Musical, Kinky Boots*. As Stage Manager / fel Rheolwr Llwyfan, *Mary Stuart* (RWCMD); as Assistant Stage Manager / fel Rheolwr Llwyfan Cynorthwyol, *Wonder of the World* (RWCMD); as / fel Flyman, *The Moors* (RWCMD); as Camera Assistant / fel Cynorthwyydd Camera, *Drive* (It's My Shout Short Film project); as Technical Stage Manager on Book / fel Rheolwr Llwyfan Technegol ar Lyfr, *Sophocles' Oedipus*, *Silent Practice* (London Academy of Dramatic Arts); as Technical Swing / fel Swing Technegol, *The Doctor* (Duke of York Theatre, London).

ANDY PIKE
Lighting Designer / Cynllunydd Goleuo

For Sherman Theatre / Ar gyfer Theatr y Sherman: *Tales of the Brothers Grimm, A Midsummer Night's Dream, Dance to the Bone, A Christmas Carol, Back in Play Festival, Lose Yourself, The Merthyr Stigmatist.*

Theatre includes / Theatr yn cynnwys: *Cherry Town Moscow* (Welsh National Opera / Opera Cenedlaethol Cymru); *Road* (Taking Flight); *Nutcracker* (Atlanta Ballet); *Company* (West End); *Y Fenyw Mewn Du, The Butterfly Hunter, Eye of the Storm* (Theatr na nÓg).

Television includes / Teledu yn cynnwys: *Strictly Come Dancing* (BBC).

Sports & Events include / Chwaraeon a Digwyddiadau yn cynnwys: *King Charles' 70th Birthday Party, Handball World Cup, Asian Games.*

TAKISHA SARGENT
Composer / Cyfansoddwr

The Women of Llanrumney marks Takisha's professional debut.

Mae *The Women of Llanrumney* yn nodi ymddangosiad proffesiynol cyntaf Takisha.

IAN BARNARD
Sound Designer / Chynllunydd Sain

For Sherman Theatre / Ar gyfer Theatr y Sherman: *Tales of the Brothers Grimm, A Midsummer Night's Dream, A Christmas Carol, The Merthyr Stigmatist, The Snow Queen, Alice in Wonderland, The Wind in the Willows, The Borrowers, The Hunting of the Snark.*

Theatre includes / Theatr yn cynnwys: *Huno* (The Other Room); *Faith* (RSC / Coventry City of Culture); *Josephine* (Theatre Royal, Bath); *The Glee Club* (Out of Joint); *Into the Light* (Hijinx / Teatro La Ribalta); *The Butterfly Hunter, The White Feather* (Theatr na nÓg); *Y Cylch Sialc, Macbeth* (Theatr Genedlaethol Cymru).

Radio/Online Drama includes / Radio/Drama arlein yn cynnwys: *We Need Bees, It'll all be over by Christmas, The Arandora Star* (Theatr na nÓg); *Young Playwrights Series 2020/21* (Theatr Iolo); *Binaural Stories* (Barnaby Southgate).

STUDIO SUPPORTERS
CEFNOGWYR Y STIWDIO

Support a very special place in Welsh theatre.

Dewch yn gefnogwr i le arbennig iawn ym myd y theatr yng Nghymru.

If any one space is the engine room of Welsh theatre, the Sherman Studio is it. Across the year the Sherman Studio is the setting for the first performances of future classics. It is where new writing takes shape and young people experience performing on stage or seeing live theatre for the first time.

By donating £200 and becoming a Studio Supporter you will be championing new writing, new voices and new possibilities.

As a thank you for your donation, your name will be added to a dedicated Studio Supporters donor board, situated in the entrance to the Sherman Studio.

Os oes unrhyw ofod yn injan i fyd theatr yng Nghymru, Stiwdio'r Sherman yw hi. Stiwdio'r Sherman yw lleoliad ar gyfer perfformiadau cyntaf clasuron y dyfodol. Dyma le mae ysgrifennu newydd craff yn cael ei ffurfio a phobl ifanc yn cael eu profiadau cyntaf o berfformio ar lwyfan neu brofi theatr byw.

Drwy gyfrannu £200 a dod yn Gefnogwr y Stiwdio byddwch yn cefnogi ysgrifennu newydd, lleisiau newydd a phosibiliadau newydd.

Fel diolch am eich rhodd, bydd eich enw yn cael ei ychwanegu at y bwrdd rhoddwyr fel Cefnogwr y Stiwdio ym mynedfa Stiwdio Theatr y Sherman.

To become a Studio Supporter today, donate online or call 02920 646900.

I ddod yn Gefnogwr y Stiwdio heddiw, cyfrannwch ar-lein neu ffoniwch 02920 646900.

THE WOMEN OF LLANRUMNEY

Azuka Oforka

We are going to emancipate ourselves from mental slavery, for though others may free the body, none but ourselves can free the mind.

Marcus Garvey

Characters

ANNIE, *fifty years old. Mixed race, Jamaican*
CERYS, *twenty-five years old. Dark skinned, Black, Jamaican. Six months pregnant*
ELISABETH MORGAN, *late forties. White, Welsh*
TOMMY FLYNN, *twenties. White, Irish*
SIMON TAYLOR, *thirties. White, Scottish-Jamaican. He speaks with a 'uptown' Jamaican accent*
MR AINSWORTH, *fifties. White, English*

Notes

A dash (–) at the end of a line indicates an interruption or unfinished thought.

One actor can play all the male parts.

This text went to press before the end of rehearsals and so may differ slightly from the play as performed.

ACT ONE

Day one.

Llanrumney plantation. Saint Mary Parish, Jamaica. 1765.

The dining room of the Great House. The room is luxuriously furnished, a portrait of Captain Henry Morgan hangs on the wall. In the centre of the room is a mahogany dinner table and chairs.

ANNIE *is roughly buttoning* CERYS *into her dress.*

ANNIE. Can't nobody say Llanrumney niggers not the best-dressed niggers inna the whole parish, mistress nah skimp when it comes to dressing her slaves.

CERYS. House slaves. Field hand lucky fi get old rag.

ANNIE. Finest muslin and the prettiest lace, everybody know a Llanrumney nigger that.

ANNIE *steps back from* CERYS.

You're ready.

ANNIE *kisses her teeth and shakes her head.*

Ready as you'll ever be. How you feel?

CERYS *tugs at her dress uncomfortably.*

CERYS. How me supposed to feel?

ANNIE. Ready!

CERYS *nods, unenthusiastically.*

CERYS. Me ready.

ANNIE. Proud. Honoured. That's how you should feel.

CERYS. Honoured? Fi wha?

ANNIE. For. What.

CERYS (*exaggerated enunciation*). For. What?

ANNIE. For the privilege to work in the Great House of the esteemed Llanrumney Estate. For the prestigious opportunity to work in such close proximity to our generous mistress. You should be proud, honoured and *grateful* that you're not out in the field cutting cane.

Again, ANNIE *kisses her teeth.*

We'll be a damn laughing stock. A field hand into a lady's maid? And one as dark as you.

ANNIE *shakes her head.*

It's unheard of.

CERYS. Yet here me stand.

ANNIE. Not if I had my way, believe me, not if I had my way.

CERYS. You didn't send fi me?

ANNIE. No. I had no choice in the matter, there's no one else. No one. Every girl me train up, she sell off. She's sold everyone.

Long beat.

You remember everything me teach you?

CERYS. Yes.

ANNIE. Then stan' up straight.

CERYS *fixes her posture.*

CERYS. Stan' straight, arms to the side or clasp together at the front, but never cross. Don't look her in she eye, don't speak.

ANNIE. Unless?

CERYS. Unless she speak to me. Serve drinks from di right, food from di left. Me remember, everything.

ANNIE. You learn fast. Good.

CERYS. A smart field hand, that shock you?

ANNIE *ignores this question.*

None are smarter.

ANNIE *laughs.*

ANNIE. Please.

CERYS *wanders around the room taking in all the grandeur.*

CERYS. All my life me never once step foot inna dis place. Overseer whip di life out of you if you just look pon di Great House.

ANNIE. As he should! Them Coromantee field niggers are nothing but trouble with their wild African ways. All them do is plot 'bout rebellion and cause nothing but trouble. Fear of the slave driver's lash is the only thing that keeps them savages in line.

CERYS. Dem don't fear the lash.

Beat.

ANNIE. So what dem fear?

CERYS *ignores this question and continues to look around the room.*

CERYS. You ever work di fields a day in your life?

ANNIE. Me?

ANNIE *laughs heartily.*

Never! A slave of my breeding, my pedigree does not work in no cane field. My father was the master of Llanrumney –

CERYS. And your muma, who was she?

ANNIE. His father and grandfather before that.

CERYS *looks up at the portrait of Captain Henry Morgan.*

CERYS. That him, your father?

ANNIE. That is the late great Captain Henry Morgan. The founder of Llanrumney Estate and Lieutenant Governor of Jamaica, *three* times over.

A founding father, fearless conquer and mighty buccaneer. He defeated the Spanish and helped create the British colony of Jamaica. A great man *and* an ancestor of mine.

CERYS. So a ancestor of mine?

ANNIE *ignores this and begins to lay the table.*

ANNIE. Teaspoon, breakfast knife, breakfast fork, napkin.

CERYS. Your ancestor be my ancestor –

ANNIE. Teaspoon –

CERYS. Right?

ANNIE. Breakfast knife –

CERYS. Breakfast fork, napkin, me remember. Everything. Never forget nothing. I remember you.

Long awkward silence.

Me remember everything she tell me about you. Miss Dilys.

ANNIE. I don't know no Dilys.

CERYS. Yes you do. Old Miss Dilys. The field nurse. Blind in one eye. The woman you dumped me with.

ANNIE *continues to lay the table.*

ANNIE. Drinking chocolate is the fashion of the day –

CERYS. I remember what she told me about you, stoosh Annie inna di Great House.

ANNIE. But the mistress insists on coffee.

CERYS. You want me fi act like me forget?

A bell rings, ANNIE *rushes to the door.*

You want me fi pretend like me nah know your my mother?

ANNIE *exits.*

Left alone, CERYS *stares at the portrait of Captain Morgan.* ANNIE *enters pushing a mahogany serving trolly laden with food.*

I said, you want me fi act like I don't know?

ANNIE *says nothing. Long beat.*

All'a dis food fi one person?

ANNIE. Yes. Food is how these planters flex them wealth, this is nothing. I've seen tables crammed so full they buckle under the weight.

ANNIE *begins to lay the food on the table.*

The mistress likes her first breakfast –

CERYS *shakes her head in disgust, unseen by* ANNIE.

CERYS (*repulsed*). First.

ANNIE *turns to* CERYS.

ANNIE. Remember, we have first breakfast, second breakfast, luncheon, dinner, tea, supper.

CERYS. This the only thing them do, eat?

ANNIE. And drink. Lord can they drink.

CERYS *helps* ANNIE *lay the food on the table.*

Miss Elisabeth don't like breakfast Creole-style, so she spares no expense importing fine things from home. A Welsh breakfast she wants, a Welsh breakfast she gets.

CERYS. Welsh her home?

ANNIE. Wales, yes.

CERYS. Near England?

ANNIE. It is England but… it's not. It's Wales. She say it's a different country and cuss out anybody that says otherwise but… them have the same King… so. I don't really understand it too tough, all I know is *here*, be them Welsh, Irish, Scotch or Englishman, on this island, they're all the same.

CERYS. Backra.

ANNIE shoots CERYS a disapproving look.

She your kin?

ANNIE. Yes.

CERYS. You have the same father?

ANNIE. No, my father had no immediate heirs. When he died he left Llanrumney to some second cousins in Monmouthshire, Elisabeth and her brother Elis. Elis travelled to Jamaica to manage the estate but yellow fever lick him down the second him stepped foot off the ship, dead within days. So, Miss Elisabeth followed in his wake and she has been here ever since. Twenty years.

CERYS. She never marry?

ANNIE. Never. Though she has had *many* a suitor and more than her fair share of proposals. But she's smart, she always says no, she knows they're only after her land. Marry her and Llanrumney is theirs. No. It's just been she and I all these years. Through thick and thin, me one, I alone have been there.

CERYS rolls her eyes.

Through thick and thin. I nursed her when she was sick, comforted her when she was scared. Laughed with her, cried with her. Her one true friend and confidant.

CERYS. Her slave.

ANNIE is about to snap a reply back at CERYS just as ELISABETH enters. ELISABETH is dressed finely but is looking rough, very hungover from the night before.

ELISABETH. That coffee better be fucking strong, Annie. Not like that shit you served up to me yesterday.

ANNIE pulls out a chair, ELISABETH sits.

ANNIE. Nuh worry about that, Miss Elisabeth, I made it fresh myself.

ELISABETH *holds up her coffee cup to be filled.* ANNIE *signals for* CERYS *to pour the coffee.*

ELISABETH. I'm dying, my head is fucking pounding.

CERYS *pours the coffee.*

ANNIE. We had a good night, did we?

ELISABETH. We did indeed, Annie, we did indeed.

ANNIE. Wonderful.

CERYS *and* ANNIE *serve* ELISABETH *breakfast.*

ELISABETH. Actually good is too plain a word to describe last night's shenanigans at Pemberton Valley Estate.

ANNIE. Ohhh, so what word would you choose?

ELISABETH. Titillating.

ANNIE. Titi… wah.

ELISABETH. Debauched.

ANNIE. Miss!

ELISABETH. When I tell you about the carrying-on at poor old Emily Evans's attempt at a sophisticated soirée, you'll die.

ANNIE. So go on, tell me nah!

ELISABETH. Well firstly, she failed.

ANNIE. No surprise there.

ELISABETH. Miserably.

ANNIE. Mhm.

ELISABETH. Sophisticated? Island-born whites wouldn't know sophistication if it jumped up and slapped them square in the face. Creole society knows not of refinement and civility, they eat like ravenous hogs, drink like porpoises and fuck like rabbits.

ELISABETH *burps, then holds up her cup.* CERYS *pours more coffee.*

ANNIE. Indeed, Miss, they are adulterous gluttons fi true.

ELISABETH. It's the climate, I'm telling you, the heat drives the men mad. Anyway, so. The table was laid all wrong for a start.

ANNIE. Unacceptable.

ELISABETH. And no amount of gaudy table decorations could conceal that little fact. No, sophisticated it was not, thank God, what a bloody bore that would have been. No, it was a scandalous exhibition of unabashed vanity and wantonness!

ANNIE. Woi!

ELISABETH. And I loved every single second of it!!

ELISABETH *burps again, then holds up a crystal glass.* ANNIE *signals for* CERYS *to serve some punch from the punch bowl at the centre of the table.*

ANNIE. The punch.

CERYS *serves the punch.*

ELISABETH. So. We are all sat for dinner, on my right was James Jenkins, owner of Llanblethian Hill plantation. Drunk on his own self-importance as per usual, bragging about investing in some new design of copper-lined sugar-boiling caldrons.

ANNIE *pretends to fall asleep, snoring.* ELISABETH *roars with laughter.*

Exactly! Blah blah, yawn yawn!!

ELISABETH *stuffs more food into her mouth and continues to talk with her mouth full.*

To my left was my darling Mary Lewis, trustee of the Wales Estate.

ANNIE. She learn how to dress yet?

ELISABETH. Nope! Still dressing like a dowdy school mistress with no money or taste.

ANNIE. What a shame, what a waste. With her fortune, the fashions she could –

ELISABETH. Also in attendance was some absentee planter just returned from Bristol, with him was his new wife. A pale, meek little thing. Barely said a word all night, grimaced and gagged at every dish that was offered.

ANNIE. How rude. No class?

ELISABETH. Well, I of all people understand it takes ones palate some time to adjust to the food here.'

ANNIE. But there is an etiquette to these things. Just pick a few things and push them around your plate all evening, or have a little taste, a little try –

ELISABETH. And then spit them into your napkin as I did.

ANNIE. Discreetly, I hope?

ELISABETH. Of course.

ANNIE. The food that bad?

ELISABETH. No, it was delicious.

ANNIE. It was? She must have a new cook then.

ELISABETH. She does.

ANNIE. Mhm.

ELISABETH. When old Mrs Cruikshank popped her clogs that spoiled brat Emily Evans swooped in and brought her renowned cook at auction, splashed her husband's cash and outbid everybody.

ANNIE. As usual.

ELISABETH. Because, as we well know, as her husband prefers the company of little mulatto house girls over her, she is left bored and alone to spend his money. Vacuous little princess, she has no substance to her life, no estate to run, no business to occupy her. He breeds a litter of quadroons –

ANNIE. She squanders his fortune.

ELISABETH. Pitiful. And of course vapid soul that she is, she spent the whole night droning on about her newly acquired cook, relentlessly going on and on, telling us that her slave had cooked for the Lieutenant Governor –

ANNIE (*impressed*). The governor?

ELISABETH. Cooked at King's house, cooked for the Attorney General. Blah blah.

Beat. ELISABETH *looks at* ANNIE, *waiting for a reaction.*

ANNIE. Yawn, yawn.

ELISABETH. The food was sublime. But as usual, there was just way too much of it. The typical ostentatious Creole display. Oysters, crabs –

ANNIE. Fried fish?

ELISABETH. Mhm, swimming in oil. Cold fish, pickled.

ANNIE. Pie?

ELISABETH. Pigeon.

ANNIE. Nice.

ELISABETH. Turtle soup, pepper pot, cold veal, roast beef, mutton chops.

ANNIE. A mighty spread.

ELISABETH. Tarts, cakes, fruits, jellies, chocolate, coffee and wine, dear God, there was so much wine.

ANNIE. All that eating and you still had time for titillation?

ELISABETH. Yes, yes, I'm getting to the titillating bit. So…

ELISABETH *stuffs more food in her mouth.*

ANNIE. So?

ELISABETH. So, across from me was a very handsome young man. Dark eyes. Dark hair.

ANNIE. Just how you like them.

ELISABETH. Exactly. His name is Rhys and his father was from my home town.

ANNIE. Ooohhh!

ELISABETH. Exactly! But sat right next to him was Edmund Ainsworth.

ANNIE. Oh lord.

ELISABETH. With his puffy red face and bloodshot eyes. An absolute killjoy, as per usual. Rhys was making eyes at me. His big. Piercing brown eyes. Looking deep into my soul, they glanced quite a few times at my cleavage too –

ANNIE. Miss Elisabeth.

ELISABETH. We were smiling, giggling and flirting, much to the vexation of old Edmund Ainsworth.

ANNIE. He loves you.

ELISABETH. His face was getting redder and redder, I thought he'd explode. Rhys and I tried to converse in our mother tongue but we were interrupted constantly by the puffy old red-faced toad who demanded we speak in English so he could understand.

ANNIE. He was jealous.

ELISABETH. So Rhys and I excused ourselves. Esgusodwch ni.

ANNIE. No, he wouldn't like that!

ELISABETH. He didn't, I honestly thought he'd explode. Rhys and I left, and. We explored. The gardens. When we were done. Exploring. We headed back and who do I turn and see –

ANNIE. The toad, the old toad!

ELISABETH. The puffy old red-faced toad, on his knees!

ANNIE. Lord Jesus.

ELISABETH. Sobbing. On his knees. Proclaiming his undying love for me / again.

ANNIE. Again.

ELISABETH. The old lush summoned Rhys to a duel.

ANNIE. No!

ELISABETH. Yes! But Rhys just laughed and walked off back to the party, left me alone with Ainsworth.

ANNIE. Not very gentlemanly.

ELISABETH. No. So I was left alone with Ainsworth, who wouldn't shut up, declaring his love and demanding my hand in marriage, again.

ANNIE. What did you say?

ELISABETH. No, of course! I said no before, I said no again and I will continue to say no every single time he asks.

ANNIE. Must feel nice to be wanted so.

ELISABETH. No, it's fucking annoying. I went back to the party, where I saw Rhys rummaging up Emily Evans's skirt.

ANNIE. In front of she husband?

ELISABETH. Oh he was passed out, but even if he was stone-cold sober he wouldn't give a shit. So, that was my night.

ELISABETH *yawns, then gives an exhausted sigh and stands up,* ANNIE *pulls out her chair.*

I need to rest.

ANNIE. Of course, miss, you must be exhausted.

ELISABETH. I'll snooze on the day bed by the veranda.

ANNIE. I'll call the boy to come fan you.

ELISABETH. No, I want to be alone.

ANNIE. Okay, I'll come fan you –

ELISABETH. No! Your creaking joints will keep me wide awake. I need to sleep, Annie. Refresh, rejuvenate. Gather myself before. (*Beat.*) Simon Taylor arrives.

ANNIE. Simon Taylor?

ELISABETH *flips her fan.*

ELISABETH. Indeed.

ANNIE. The Simon Taylor. Of Lyssons Estate?

ELISABETH *fans herself.*

ELISABETH. Yes.

ANNIE *grins at* ELISABETH, *who is trying to remain composed and not grin back.*

He'll be joining me for second breakfast.

ANNIE. Just. The two of you?

Smiling, ELISABETH *fans herself*

ELISABETH. Yes.

ANNIE. Miss Elisabeth.

ELISABETH. He sent word that he was in Saint Mary and requested the pleasure of my company.

ANNIE. He is an elite man.

ELISABETH. Indeed.

ANNIE. Moves in elite circles.

ELISABETH. Indeed. Of course, I said it would be an honour and a pleasure to host him.

ANNIE. Of course.

ELISABETH. Emily Evans will choke when she finds out. No longer will I be forced to suffer the monotony of Saint Mary's vapid plantocracy, now I am moving with a higher class of people. The richest man on the island, Annie. Inherited his father's many estates, sent to school at Eton, he went to school with princes. Princes, Annie. A gentleman, a landed gentleman!

ELISABETH *squeals in excitement as she exits.* ANNIE *turns to* CERYS.

ANNIE. See that. Her one true friend and confidant.

CERYS. Me never see that. No.

ANNIE. So what you see?

CERYS. Her slave. Her most loyal slave, that loves her mistress more than she loves her own damn self.

ANNIE *scoffs*.

A fool that don't even know she's a slave, that's what me see.

ANNIE *starts to clear the table*.

You think you free?

ANNIE. No, not yet, but I will be.

CERYS *laughs*.

I'm no fool, Cerys. I am a very very smart woman. The closer you are to white people the closer you are to freedom, it's only a matter of time until she writes my manumission papers and frees me.

CERYS. That's not freedom. Real freedom is fought for. Rebellion –

ANNIE *slaps* CERYS *hard around the face*.

ANNIE. Don't say that word in here! Ever. Never say that word again.

ACT TWO

ANNIE *and* CERYS *are laying the table for 'second breakfast'.*

Offstage: We hear ELISABETH *roar with laughter as she approaches.*

ANNIE *and* CERYS *stop laying the table and stand to attention, arms clasped in front of them.*

Enter ELISABETH *and* SIMON TAYLOR.

ELISABETH. Witty and debonair, what a treat!

SIMON TAYLOR. You flatter me.

ELISABETH. I mean every word and a very rare treat at that. Good conversation with distinguished company is hard to find in the hills of Saint Mary.

SIMON TAYLOR. I was shocked, I must say, to learn you live alone up here. I thought you'd rent a little town house in Kingston and pay someone to run this place for you. Most distinguished ladies that reside in Jamaica alone, live in a little town house in Kingston.

ELISABETH. I am a rural girl at heart.

SIMON TAYLOR. Saint Mary is no safe place for a single woman, between the Marrons in Scott's Hall and those murderers who evaded capture after Tacky's failed rebellion, this mountainous terrain is too dark and too dangerous for a woman to reside alone, Miss Morgan.

ELISABETH *flips her fan and fans herself.*

ELISABETH. You're concerned for my wellbeing, Mr Taylor?

SIMON TAYLOR. Of course.

ELISABETH. I love it up here, the hills and mountains remind me of home.

SIMON TAYLOR. Monmouthshire.

ELISABETH. Yes. You've done your research on me.

SIMON TAYLOR. Yes.

ELISABETH *smiles, a flirtatious smile.*

ELISABETH. You must be hungry. Please, sit.

ANNIE *and* CERYS *pull out two chairs.* SIMON TAYLOR *and* ELISABETH *sit.*

We've turtle soup, pepper pot, cold veal, roast beef. Pie, pigeon.

SIMON TAYLOR. You've spared no expense, I see.

ELISABETH. Please. Mr Taylor.

SIMON TAYLOR. Simon.

ELISABETH *smiles.*

ELISABETH. Simon, it's crass to talk about money at the table.

ELISABETH *signals for* ANNIE *to serve some punch.*

Some rum and lime punch.

ANNIE *goes to serve the punch.*

SIMON TAYLOR (*to* ANNIE). No. (*To* ELISABETH.) None for me, thank you. I don't drink rum –

ELISABETH. A Creole man who doesn't drink rum?

SIMON TAYLOR. An anomaly, no?

ELISABETH. Indeed.

ELISABETH *drinks her punch.*

SIMON TAYLOR. I don't drink rum in the day and certainly not for breakfast.

ELISABETH *puts her glass down.*

ELISABETH. But you indulge once night falls?

ANNIE *goes to fill up* ELISABETH*'s glass,* ELISABETH *shoos her away.*

SIMON TAYLOR. A little. I need a clear head come morning, most days I've usually done four, sometimes five hours of business before nine a.m.

ELISABETH. A dedicated and ambitious man. Impressive.

SIMON TAYLOR. So one glass, occasionally, very rarely two. Very rarely.

ELISABETH. You wake up at five?

SIMON TAYLOR. Yes.

ELISABETH. In the morning?

SIMON TAYLOR. It's the right thing to do, the proper thing to do. People flock to this island under pretences of quick and easy wealth, but there is nothing easy about sugar, Miss Morgan.

ELISABETH. Elisabeth, please.

SIMON TAYLOR. There is nothing easy about agriculture, Elisabeth. It demands dedication, planning, management. With all these things you can reap great rewards. But without them. Complacency. Complacency will always lead to ruin. I've seen it many times. Many times.

ELISABETH *signals to* ANNIE *to fill her glass with punch.* ANNIE *does so.*

ELISABETH. All work and no play?

ELISABETH *smiles.*

It's important. Play. Recreational pursuits. They're important, Simon.

SIMON TAYLOR. Go on then, I'll have a small drop. A very small drop.

ANNIE *pours him a small drop of punch.*

That's enough.

ELISABETH *raises her glass to toast.*

ELISABETH. Cheers.

SIMON TAYLOR *doesn't join her in a toast, instead he lifts his glass to his nose and smells it. Then he takes a sip, swooshing it around in his mouth for quite a while before swallowing.*

Beat. SIMON TAYLOR *nods in satisfaction.*

SIMON TAYLOR. Nice.

ELISABETH. We Morgans of Llanrumney take our rum very seriously. Our estate is one of the oldest in Jamaica. After a lifetime of swashbuckling at sea, Captain Morgan settled here, lay claim to the land and called it Llanrumney after his place of birth. The land was deep and fertile, ripe for cultivating sugar cane to make molasses and we've been turning molasses into rum ever since. He was a pioneer in settlement, at taming this wild land.

SIMON TAYLOR. He was.

ELISABETH. Simon, I have to say I am really touched by your visit. Your company today means a great deal to me. More than you could ever know. Jamaica is seen as the Eldorado of the British colonies, the jewel in the crown of the empire, but –

SIMON TAYLOR. All that glisters is not gold.

ELISABETH. We both know this is a ruthless and unrelentingly cruel island. A disease ridden suburb of hell. (*Beat.*) It's a brutal land, that often feels impossible to survive.

SIMON TAYLOR. Which is why most planters are absentees, Miss Elisabeth. They run home within a matter of weeks and leave the running of their plantations to stronger, more business-minded *men* like me. The sodom of the Indies. That's what they call Jamaica back home in their papers and pamphlets.

ELISABETH *laughs.*

ELISABETH. They look down on us and our island ways but those pompous, pious hypocrites still eat our sugar, drink our rum and send their children to school in the buildings our money built.

SIMON TAYLOR. There's truth to it though, the sodom of the Indies, a lot of truth. This island is a haven for drunkards, thieves and harlots. No place for a white woman. It is a reckless land with a lawless spirit.

SIMON TAYLOR *looks up at the portrait of Captain Henry Morgan.*

But any country founded by pirates, would be. We're a colony born from King-killing Cromwellian pirates who looted this land from the Spanish. Their legacy of treachery and territorial theft still lives on today.

ELISABETH. Are you sure I can't tempt you to a drop more punch?

SIMON TAYLOR. No, no.

ELISABETH. You liked the rum?

SIMON TAYLOR. It was good. Bright, nectary.

ELISABETH. Our latest batch.

SIMON TAYLOR. Your last batch, that's why I am here.

ELISABETH. Our latest batch, yes.

SIMON TAYLOR. Last. This will be your last ever batch, Miss Morgan. Elisabeth. Your crop has failed.

ELISABETH. My crop has... no.

SIMON TAYLOR. You didn't know that?

ELISABETH. No.

Long beat.

What?

SIMON TAYLOR. Your crop has failed.

ELISABETH *laughs*.

ELISABETH. If that were true, Mr Taylor, how would you know before me?

SIMON TAYLOR. Because your life revolves around society parties, you drink yourself into oblivion every night and your days are dedicated to recovering from the night before. My days, as I said, are dedicated to business, business is my life and I make it a priority to not only know the runnings of my own estates but that of my competitors. And because you don't pay your bookkeepers and overseers –

ELISABETH. I pay them –

SIMON TAYLOR. Not fairly and definitely not on time. They moonlight on other estates, my estates and they are quick to vent their frustrations and share your business. Your crop has failed. Disease has set into your soil, a fungal rot has and will contaminate every stem of cane that sprouts. Sugar cane is a perennial grass, which means –

ELISABETH. Don't patronise me, Mr Taylor. I am an intelligent and educated woman, I know what perennial means.

SIMON TAYLOR. It means?

ELISABETH. It means. My next crop will fail.

SIMON TAYLOR. Correct. But there is a way to fix this problem.

Beat.

ELISABETH. How?

SIMON TAYLOR. You are an intelligent and educated woman, you tell me.

Silence.

How? How can this problem be fixed?

ELISABETH. Remove all remaining crops, destroy them.

SIMON TAYLOR. Burn them, yes. Then what will you do?

ELISABETH. Dry out the rotten soil, plough every field, constantly rotate the soil to expose it to the sun. I am from a farming family, I –

SIMON TAYLOR. How long will that take, no new crops can be planted until your rotten soil is healthy. How long will that take?

Silence.

Years, two is my guess. It will cost you time and money, two things you have very little of, Elisabeth.

ELISABETH. Excuse me.

SIMON TAYLOR. You live way beyond your means, shopping, gambling. You rack up debt wherever you go –

ELISABETH. How dare you –

SIMON TAYLOR. The profits from the sugar and rum produced by your crops allowed you to keep the wolf from the door.

Constantly paying your debtors instead of investing in your land. Constantly robbing Peter to pay Paul. But now you can't rob Peter. How you going to pay Paul?

ELISABETH. This is why you're here?

SIMON TAYLOR. No crop, no sugar.

ELISABETH. Is this why you came?

SIMON TAYLOR. No sugar, no money.

ELISABETH. I have assets –

SIMON TAYLOR. Your disease-ridden land is your only asset –

ELISABETH. Why are you here, Mr Taylor, get to the fucking point!

SIMON TAYLOR. I am here with a solution.

ELISABETH. Go on.

SIMON TAYLOR. An answer to your prayers.

ELISABETH. Spit it out.

SIMON TAYLOR. Sell up.

ANNIE. Miss.

SIMON TAYLOR. Sell to me.

ANNIE. No, miss.

ELISABETH. Hush.

ANNIE. You can't.

SIMON TAYLOR. Shut up.

ELISABETH. Annie, please.

SIMON TAYLOR. The soil up here is rich and fertile, Llanrumney has the potential to be one of the most prosperous estates in Jamaica. I have the money and the expertise to transform this place.

ELISABETH. Territorial theft.

SIMON TAYLOR *laughs*.

SIMON TAYLOR. No, I'm not a thieving pirate out to steal your land. I am willing to pay you enough, more than it's worth, to settle your debts and return to Wales somewhat of a wealthy woman.

ELISABETH. I don't want to go back to Wales.

SIMON TAYLOR. I've no doubt you will miss the autonomy women enjoy out here but you can't stay here. You're facing financial ruin. Destitution.

ELISABETH *stands*.

ELISABETH. No. I'd like you to leave.

SIMON TAYLOR *stands*.

SIMON TAYLOR. It's only a matter of days before your creditors come knocking, Elisabeth.

ELISABETH. Please leave.

SIMON TAYLOR. Dear lady, please do not let your emotions cloud –

ELISABETH. Get out!

SIMON TAYLOR *walks to the door.*

SIMON TAYLOR. My offer stands if you change your mind. Good luck.

SIMON TAYLOR *exits*.

ELISABETH *paces anxiously*.

ANNIE. Miss? Miss Elisabeth? You never knew things so bad? How? How you never knew things so bad?

ELISABETH. Stop buzzing in my ear like a fucking mosquito! Shut up! Shut up and let me think for the love of God, shut up!

ELISABETH *storms out*.

ANNIE: How?

Silence. ANNIE *paces, panicking.* CERYS *is calm, surveying the leftover food.*

CERYS. All'a this food just waste.

ANNIE. How?

CERYS. In my whole life –

ANNIE. How she never knew things got so bad?

CERYS. Me never seen so much food.

CERYS *pokes and prods at some of the leftovers*.

ANNIE. Every girl me train up she sell off. She sold everybody.

CERYS. People starving out there and all'a this food just waste.

ANNIE. If her creditors come, they take everything, me.

CERYS. Yes.

CERYS *picks at the leftover food*.

ANNIE. If she sells Llanrumney, she sells me.

CERYS. That's how it goes, yes.

CERYS *picks up a bread roll*.

ANNIE. They'll take me, along with everything else to settle her debts. They'll take me.

CERYS *smells the bread roll.*

CERYS. Yes, along with all her other property. The crockery, the cutlery, the horses and the hogs. That's how slavery go.

ANNIE. Sell me to God knows where.

CERYS *slowly nibbles at the bread roll, apprehensive of its taste.*

Made to start again. Lose my position, my privilege.

CERYS *likes the taste of the bread roll, eats more.*

CERYS. Made to work the field.

ANNIE. After coming so far, so close to freedom, to peace. If they come take me before she gives me my papers –

CERYS. Freedom can't be written on no piece of paper. Freedom can't be handed from one person to another on no piece of paper, that's not real freedom.

CERYS *picks up a slice of cake,* ANNIE *sees this, slaps the cake out of* CERYS *hands.*

ANNIE. Don't touch their food! We never touch their food, we never touch anything of theirs unless we're ordered to.

CERYS *picks the cake back up and eats it.* ANNIE *freezes, staggered by this act of disobedience.*

Are you crazy?

CERYS. Are you?

ANNIE. You are. You're crazy.

CERYS. Real freedom is fought for through revolution and war –

ANNIE. Lord Jesus.

ANNIE *backs away from* CERYS.

CERYS. Real freedom is taken, demanded by all for the benefit of all.

ANNIE. Mad girl.

CERYS. You really want to be free?

Beat.

You have a chance at true freedom, do you really want to be free, truly free?

Longer beat.

ANNIE. Yes.

CERYS. War is coming –

ANNIE. No.

ANNIE backs away from CERYS. ELISABETH enters sobbing.

ELISABETH. I've really made a mess of all this, Annie.

ANNIE. Miss Elisabeth –

ELISABETH. I've ruined everything.

ANNIE. Breathe.

ELISABETH. Gambled away a legacy.

ANNIE. No, no –

ELISABETH hyperventilates.

Please, miss. Calm down, breathe.

ELISABETH. I've lost it all.

ANNIE. No.

ELISABETH. Ruined.

ANNIE. We'll fix this.

ELISABETH. I'm ruined.

ANNIE. Miss. Please.

ELISABETH. How will I ever show my face in society again, the shame!

ANNIE. We have to fix this.

ELISABETH. They'll all whisper and gossip, they'll all laugh at me. Elisabeth Morgan carted away to debtors' prison. The humiliation. Destitute and penniless. They'll have so much fun with this!

ANNIE. Enough!

Shocked, ELISABETH *stops crying.*

What good is crying going to do us. No amount of tears is going to get us out of this trouble we've got ourselves in. Please breathe!

ELISABETH. I've lost it.

ANNIE. No.

ELISABETH. I've lost Llanrumney.

ANNIE. You give up too easy.

ELISABETH. What choice do I have, what else can I do?

ANNIE. Fight! Llanrumney is your birthright, your heritage, fight for it. If they take Llanrumney, they take me, along with all your other property to settle your debts. I need you to fight.

ELISABETH. What can I do?

Beat.

ANNIE. Ask Mr Ainsworth. He's in love with you.

ELISABETH *grimaces in disgust.*

Ask him for the money you need, all of it.

ELISABETH. I can't.

ANNIE. You have to. He'll give you whatever you ask. Ask him.

ELISABETH. I can't.

ANNIE. He's a very wealthy man, he won't miss the money, ask him.

ELISABETH. I can't! Because I've already asked him for money, lots of money.

ANNIE. And he gave it to you?

ELISABETH. Yes.

ANNIE. And you spend it?

ELISABETH *becomes tearful again*.

ELISABETH. Yes.

ANNIE. Ask for more.

ELISABETH. I can't! He won't give me another penny until I give him my hand in... No! No, I won't marry that rancid old walrus, I won't do it!

ANNIE. He'll save Llanrumney, he'll save us, we can stay and nothing at all will change!

ELISABETH *hyperventilates*.

ELISABETH. Oh God.

ANNIE. What other choices do we have?!

ELISABETH *sobs*.

ELISABETH. Oh God.

ANNIE *pours* ELISABETH *a shot of rum and passes it to her.*

ANNIE. Okay, okay.

ELISABETH *backs the shot*.

No Mr Ainsworth.

ELISABETH *calms down. Long beat*.

Mr Flynn?

ELISABETH. Who?

ANNIE. Young Tommy Flynn.

Long beat as ELISABETH *tries hard to remember.*

ELISABETH. Who?

ANNIE. Irish boy was in servitude here for many years.

ELISABETH *grimaces in disgust.*

ELISABETH. An indentured servant?

ANNIE. He's a rich man now.

Beat.

ELISABETH. He is?

ANNIE. Oh yes, flashy with it too. As soon he earned his freedom and his seven years were up, he bought Alice. You don't remember?

ELISABETH. No.

ANNIE. Alice?

ELISABETH *shakes her head.*

ELISABETH. No.

ANNIE. Mulatto house slave, she worked in the cook house. He'd saved all those years for her, he said. Had a thing for her, an obsession. When he left, he bought her with the money he'd made from hustling in Port Maria. She bore him three children, two girls, twins and a boy. He sold them, and then he sold her and with that money, he bought a small plot of land, harvested sugar cane and he's been on the rise ever since. Owns and manages several plantations all across the island. Send for him.

ELISABETH. I will.

ANNIE *walks to a chest of drawers, pulls it open and takes out some writing paper and a pen.*

ANNIE. Ask him for a loan.

ANNIE *passes the paper to* ELISABETH. ELISABETH *starts to head out of the room to begin writing.*

ELISABETH. Good old…

ELISABETH *stops and turns back to* ANNIE *for a prompt.*

ANNIE. TOMMY FLYNN.

ELISABETH. Good old Tommy Flynn, so glad he's done so well.

ELISABETH *leaves with pen and paper. Silence.*

CERYS. War is coming. All across the island soldiers are ready, waiting. Men, women, old and young all joined together. We're planning to –

ANNIE. We? You?

CERYS. Yes. On the night of the last visible crescent of the waning moon, when the sky is dark, the sound of a conch-shell horn will ring out three times, and that is our sign, our signal, to rise up in rebellion.

ANNIE. Cerys, I warned you, never –

CERYS. Hundreds of us, Akan, Ashanti, Igbos, island-born captives. All'a we together, marching and chanting with one voice, ye nye nkowa bio –

ANNIE *kisses her teeth in disgust.*

Ye nye nkowa bio. We be slaves no more. They're outnumbered, together we can overthrow them. United we can start our own nation, a free Black... African nation.

ANNIE. You too fool-fool, this ain't Africa. Y'nah African, stupid girl!

CERYS. The leaders of our rebellion –

ANNIE *goes to slap* CERYS *around her face but* CERYS *dodges her reach.*

Our leaders are. Kofi is a Akan chief, his master thinks he's just some dumb carriage driver, but he is the smartest and bravest, he goes from plantation to plantation organising our army. Queen Akua, or Jenny that's what they call her at Trinity Estate, she is an Ashanti warrior. Africa lives within them. It lives within –

ANNIE *kisses her teeth again.*

ANNIE. My father beat me close to death when I got pregnant with you, for breeding without his permission.

Then he got the overseers to beat me, then he got the old bitch housekeeper to beat me some more. I was amazed you didn't die inside me. When I went into labour I was sure you'd be born cold and still but you survived unharmed, or so I thought. They clearly mashed up your head. It's obvious your brain ain't right.

Beat.

CERYS. So you're admitting, you're my –

ANNIE. Tacky was a warlord, some big Africa chief and look what they did to him when he caused all that trouble. They chopped his head off and left it on a pike to rot for us all to see what would happen to us if we dared to think them same troublesome thoughts. Is that what you want?

CERYS. Me want freedom, rebellion is our only chance –

ANNIE. Chance at what, death?! Slow torturous death? That's all that comes from rebellion and war. You know how many times in my life I've witnessed slave rebellions fail, how many times in my life I have seen the bloody aftermath? Watched bodies be bludgeoned to an unrecognisable pulp, drawn and quartered, burned alive. My own mother had the same foolish, dangerous thoughts as you and they killed her for it.

CERYS. Your mother?

ANNIE. Yes. (*Beat.*) Them born free negros the worst.

CERYS. My grandmother was born free?

Beat.

ANNIE. Yes.

CERYS. Where? Tell me about her. I want to know.

Long beat.

ANNIE. She. She was Igbo. Beautiful. Beautiful, terracotta brown skin.

CERYS *is moved close to tears by this revelation.*

CERYS. I'm Igbo. (*Beat.*) What was her name?

ANNIE *is uncomfortable and hesitates.*

What was her name?

ANNIE. Elen. That's what they called her here, but before that, Amaka. She was ten when they brought her to Jamaica.

CERYS. She was ten when they teefed her from her home.

Beat.

ANNIE. Always spirited they say. She was always in some kinda mix-up, even from young. She would never do as she was told and was constantly whipped for impudence, they say even as the overseer thrashed her back to shreds she would struggle and cuss him out. The overseer was intent on beating her into submission, but she would always resist. I'm sure the overseer would have whipped her to death if it wasn't for the master.

CERYS. Your father?

ANNIE. He took a liking to her pretty face and terracotta-brown skin and moved her into the Great House. She could have been a favourite if she kept sweet. She could have had an easier, longer life. But she continued to cuss and struggle. She plotted, like you, plotted with others to kill the master, poison his food, burn the estate to the ground and run away into the mountains. But her plot was discovered. I was six years old. They put her in a cage, hung it from a tree. Left her there.

I was brought every day to see her, to look at her, not to speak to her or comfort her, just to watch her starve to death. The master wanted me to understand, to see the consequences of treachery. She was trapped tightly, naked, in that cage, quietly defiant but I could see the sadness in her eyes. Every day I was marched from the Great House to go and gawp at her. She was left there in the blazing heat, rain and storms. Day after day. Day after day, I was made to watch her get weaker and weaker. The sadness in her eyes turned to sorrow. Her quiet defiance turned into an anguished lament. Then one day I was dragged to see her, and a crowd had gathered around her. I thought, thank God, that's it, she's dead. And I was glad because I thought this ordeal was over. But no, she was alive, just. Alive and covered in molasses, someone... the overseer no doubt, had thrown boiling molasses over her and... all the insects and creatures that sugar attracts were swarming, eating her alive. She was too weak to scream or bat them away, she just sat there still and sorrowful. I remember wishing death upon her, praying for death to take her, willing her to hurry up and die so this all could be over. I remember the relief I felt when I heard the whispers that she had finally died. I thought they'd take her down and bury her in the pit they throw every other dead nigger in, but no. They left her to. I was taken to. Every day, to watch her rot away, for months until she was nothing but skull and bones. They left her remains up there for years in that cage. An example of the consequences of treachery.

That's all resisting and rebelling brings, more cruelty, more death.

CERYS. Me tek death over a lifetime of this. If the choice is slavery or death, then me welcome death with a smile and open arms.

ANNIE. You want to die like that?

CERYS. We live like that, sun up to sun down, cruelty and death. Every day of our lives from we babies. Not one second in we mothers' arms. From we babies they raise us like cattle, less than cattle, less than dog. No kindness, no care. From we babies. You don't know, you never cared to know but I was four years old when they put me to work in the fields. Four years old. Made to work as hard as fully grown men and women. They whipped me for carrying buckets of drinking water too slow, kicked me for digging holes too slow, punched me for trenching land too slow. Four years old. No mother to cry to. No comfort. Many of my friends died around me, many pickney. No childhood, just cruelty and death. Every day of our lives is cruelty and –

ANNIE. Not here. Not in this house with this mistress. You're not outside in the fields any more, you don't have to burn the island to the ground to live free from all that pain. You're in the house and in this house we can work the system, manipulate the system in to giving you privilege, security and safety. And she will.

Long beat.

But you have to forget all them dangerous thoughts about rebellion and war. I can keep you safe, inside this house, I can keep you both safe. And one day I can get all of us free.

ANNIE *places a hand on* CERYS*'s pregnant belly.*

All of us. But you have to forget them dangerous thoughts.

ACT THREE

Scene One

The next day.

The veranda. ELISABETH *is fast asleep in a chair, snoring.*

Enter TOMMY FLYNN, *he is dressed to the nines and reeks of new money. He watches* ELISABETH *as she sleeps. Then he creeps closer, careful not to wake her. He picks at some of the food on the table next to her and eats it. He goes to grab some more but* ELISABETH *wakes up, she is startled by his presence and screams in panic.*

TOMMY FLYNN. No, Miss Morgan –

ELISABETH. Who are you?

TOMMY FLYNN. Tommy, don't panic please, it's me, Tommy Flynn.

ELISABETH. How long have you been stood there?

TOMMY FLYNN. Not long.

ELISABETH. Stood over me... watching me sleep like some kind of pervert.

TOMMY FLYNN *laughs.*

TOMMY FLYNN. Not at all.

ELISABETH. Then why didn't you wake me?

TOMMY FLYNN. Ah, you looked so peaceful, is all.

TOMMY FLYNN *pours himself a drink.*

ELISABETH. Please, help yourself.

TOMMY FLYNN. What were you dreaming about?

ELISABETH. I beg your pardon?

TOMMY FLYNN. You had a smile on your lips. Sweet dreams, ay?

ELISABETH. Mr Flynn. That is a very inappropriate question for a gentleman to ask a lady.

TOMMY FLYNN *laughs loudly.*

TOMMY FLYNN. Don't let me fine threads fool ya, I'm no gentleman. And you're a farmer's daughter from the valleys of South Wales, so let's drop the airs and graces, shall we. It was friendly small talk, that's all.

Beat.

ELISABETH. Home. I was dreaming of home.

TOMMY FLYNN. Homesick?

ELISABETH. No. It's just the view, the rolling hills, the mountains remind me of home. I fell asleep thinking of home and found myself dreaming a nostalgic little dream of home. I don't miss it enough to return though. Do you?

TOMMY FLYNN. I don't remember much about the old country. Llanrumney I remember very well though.

ELISABETH. Have you missed it?

TOMMY FLYNN. You don't remember me at all, do you?

ELISABETH. Of course I do. Tommy Flynn.

TOMMY FLYNN. You didn't recognise me –

ELISABETH. You've changed, grown. Of course I remember you, you were a bound boy in servitude for… seven years wasn't it?

TOMMY FLYNN *nods.*

And now you are a free man, a man of standing. A wealthy business man, you've done so well.

ELISABETH *smiles.*

TOMMY FLYNN. That's the first smile I've ever had off you, I don't think you ever once looked me in the eye.

ELISABETH. You were a bound boy, Tommy. The lady of the land does not mix with the help, bookkeepers and overseers occasionally yes, but you were an indentured servant. And now you're not. (*Beat.*) The reason that I wrote to you –

TOMMY FLYNN *points into the distance.*

TOMMY FLYNN. That's where my shack was, behind that grove of palm trees. There. See it there. Stick house with a dirt floor, no furniture, straw bed. And now I'm up here in the Great House, dressed in silk and drinking punch with the mistress. Can you believe it?

ELISABETH. Yes, Jamaica is an island where vast fortunes can be made, and lost. Which is exactly why I asked you to meet me, I appreciate you coming here so promptly –

TOMMY FLYNN. Jumped at the chance.

ELISABETH. As my letter stated, it really is a matter of –

TOMMY FLYNN. The view from up here is amazing.

ELISABETH. Yes. I love it.

TOMMY FLYNN. The Great House of Llanrumney. I don't remember it looking like this.

ELISABETH. It's a little run-down, weather worn.

TOMMY FLYNN. Smaller. So much smaller than I remember.

ELISABETH. Well, you were a boy back then.

TOMMY FLYNN. It seemed like a massive palace, this place back then. And you swanned about your palace like a queen. And now –

ELISABETH. I am just a humble woman –

TOMMY FLYNN *laughs.*

TOMMY FLYNN. There's nothing humble about you, look at the clothes you're wearing.

ELISABETH. I'm a humble woman… who just happens to be dressed in the latest silk brocade imported from London –

TOMMY FLYNN. I import my clothes from London too!

TOMMY FLYNN shows off his outfit.

Lined with horsehair and backed with silk –

ELISABETH. Tommy.

TOMMY FLYNN strikes a pose, one hand on hip, chin in the air.

TOMMY FLYNN. It's Mr Flynn now.

ELISABETH. Mr Flynn. I need your help.

Beat.

TOMMY FLYNN. You need money?

ELISABETH. Yes.

TOMMY FLYNN. You need a loan.

ELISABETH. Yes, how did you know?

TOMMY FLYNN. I am smart man –

ELISABETH. I need a sizeable amount –

TOMMY FLYNN. Despite my lowly start in life, I'm a very smart man.

ELISABETH. I don't doubt that. The terms of loan –

TOMMY FLYNN. Do you remember the overseer Graham Campbell.

ELISABETH. Yes, yes I do.

TOMMY FLYNN does the sign of the cross.

TOMMY FLYNN. God bless that man, God bless his soul. Taught me to read, gave me an education, taught me my trade –

ELISABETH. The terms of the loan are yours to choose, I'd just ask for them to be fair, a crippling interest rate would –

TOMMY FLYNN. I'm smart because it was obvious from your letter that you were in a desperate situation.

ELISABETH. Well, you're right, I am.

TOMMY FLYNN. You swanned about this place like a queen and looked down on us serfs, us poor whites, you couldn't stand us Irish. Hated us the most. I remember that well.

ELISABETH. It wasn't personal –

TOMMY FLYNN. Just how it goes –

ELISABETH. Yes.

TOMMY FLYNN. Just the way it is.

ELISABETH. Yes.

TOMMY FLYNN. Yeah… you inviting me into your palace, your majesty, screams of desperation.

ELISABETH. I've admitted, yes, I am in a desperate situation.

TOMMY FLYNN. And then arriving here.

TOMMY FLYNN shakes his head.

ELISABETH. What?

TOMMY FLYNN. The place is in complete disarray. A shambles. You need me.

ELISABETH. Yes, I do.

TOMMY FLYNN. You need me desperately.

ELISABETH. Yes, Mr Flynn, I really do. I am proposing –

TOMMY FLYNN. Proposing, to me? I do!

TOMMY FLYNN laughs hysterically. ELISABETH stares at him, straight faced.

Sorry, go on.

ELISABETH. I am proposing a thirty-six-month repayment schedule, with… if you agree to these terms, a year's respite interest-free.

TOMMY FLYNN *sniggers*.

The respite, interest-free or not, gives me time to generate some income as I can't plant sugar cane any more, I –

TOMMY FLYNN. You can't plant sugar cane any more?

ELISABETH. No. Fungal rot.

TOMMY FLYNN *winces*.

TOMMY FLYNN. Damn.

ELISABETH. A year will buy me time to set up some other streams of income, livestock… a chicken farm maybe.

TOMMY FLYNN. How much do you need?

ELISABETH. Twenty thousand –

TOMMY FLYNN *shrieks*.

TOMMY FLYNN. You're gonna need a lot of fucking chickens. Twenty thousand?!

ELISABETH. Yes, I told you I am in a desperate situation. I am days away from losing Llanrumney.

TOMMY FLYNN. Twenty thousand.

TOMMY FLYNN *shakes his head and whistles at a very high pitch*.

ELISABETH. You don't have it?

TOMMY FLYNN. I've got it. I'm a very rich man.

ELISABETH. To spare –

TOMMY FLYNN. I'm a very rich man, I've got that, I've got much more than that to spare –

ELISABETH. So can you loan me that amount on the terms I put forward.

TOMMY FLYNN. I mean…

Silence as TOMMY FLYNN *thinks*.

ELISABETH. Llanrumney is at stake, Mr Flynn.

TOMMY FLYNN. Hmmm.

ELISABETH. Llanrumney is at risk, your childhood home. Does that not move you?

TOMMY FLYNN *thinks, looking at* ELISABETH.

TOMMY FLYNN. I am moved, yes.

ELISABETH. Good.

TOMMY FLYNN. By you.

ELISABETH. By my plight?

TOMMY FLYNN. By you. Stirred.

Long beat.

There are hardly any white women on this island.

ELISABETH. There are very few white people –

TOMMY FLYNN. The way you flounced around. It would get all of us pumped up.

ELISABETH. Mr Flynn.

TOMMY FLYNN. But you knew that, don't play shy you knew that. We'd watch you –

ELISABETH. Let's stick to business.

TOMMY FLYNN. Okay.

ELISABETH. Thank you.

TOMMY FLYNN. My offer. Is. One night.

ELISABETH. Excuse me?

TOMMY FLYNN. One night. Me and you. Twenty thousand.

ELISABETH *slaps* TOMMY FLYNN.

Satisfy my boyhood fantasy.

ELISABETH. How dare you.

ACT THREE, SCENE TWO   45

TOMMY FLYNN. Twenty thousand, all the money you need.

ELISABETH. I am not a whore.

ELISABETH *goes to slap* TOMMY FLYNN *again, but he grabs her hand and holds it tight, he smiles...*

TOMMY FLYNN. No repayment, no interest, one night.

ELISABETH. I'd like you to leave. Now.

TOMMY FLYNN *kisses her hand.*

TOMMY FLYNN. Think about it.

TOMMY FLYNN *exits.* ELISABETH *shouts after him.*

ELISABETH. Get off my land!

Scene Two

The dining room. ANNIE *and* CERYS *are cleaning the room and polishing flatware.*

CERYS. Everyone's talking about your mistress. Many rumblings.

ANNIE. Who?

CERYS. Everybody.

ANNIE. Who is everybody, who's running their mouth about the mistress?

CERYS. Every captive on this land.

ANNIE *falls to her knees and holds her hands up the heavens in prayer.*

ANNIE. Lord Jesus. Father God. I beseech you on my knees, shut this girl's rass –

CERYS. Every captive on this land is talking about your mistress and her debt. About Simon Taylor and his offer, it's spread like fire that he's buying Llanrumney. The people are worried, they're scared and they're angry. You know what life is like on a Taylor plantation?

ANNIE. No.

Beat.

What's life like on a Taylor plantation?

CERYS. Hell. He's the richest man on this island for a reason, he has hundreds and hundreds of captives and he works them all within an inch of their lives. And then there's Thistlewood.

Beat.

ANNIE. Thistlewood?

CERYS. Thomas Thistlewood.

ELISABETH *storms in.*

ANNIE. Miss? You get the money?

ELISABETH. That jumped-up little freckled bastard propositioned me like I was a whore.

ANNIE. But did you get the money?

ELISABETH. Did you not hear what I just said, are you fucking deaf? He propositioned me! Talked to me like I was some back-alley harlot.

ANNIE. How so?

ELISABETH. Offered me the money I need in exchange for the use of my *vagina* for a night, twenty thousand to fuck me!

ANNIE. And you said no?

ELISABETH. Are you fucking serious?

ANNIE *sighs.*

ANNIE. You said no.

ELISABETH. Of course I said no!

ANNIE. Easy money that.

ELISABETH. Annie?!

ANNIE. One night?

ELISABETH. Annie. Listen to yourself.

ANNIE. Miss Elisabeth.

ELISABETH. Prostitution?!

ANNIE. But –

ELISABETH. I would never!

ANNIE. But you've… please, pardon my impudence, miss. But you've slept with many a man pon this island. *Many* many a man.

ELISABETH. Out of choice!!

ANNIE. You have a choice. One night to save all this or lose it all and return to Wales a debt-ridden failure.

ELISABETH. What the fuck kind of choice is that?

ANNIE. It's a choice. A choice born from very little choices but it's a choice nonetheless. A position I've been forced into many many many times in my life. I just closed my eyes and forced my mind elsewhere. You'll just have to close your eyes –

ELISABETH. Annie –

ANNIE. And force your mind elsewhere.

ELISABETH. I can't do that.

ANNIE. You have to, or you have to return back home, back on the ship, back on that wretched journey you hated so much, months at sea, steerage.

ELISABETH. Heaven forbid.

ANNIE. You'll have to return back home to the people and place you hated, not as a rich Jamaica Lady but as a penniless, childless spinster with nothing but shame and a scandalised name.

ELISABETH *cringes at the thought.*

ELISABETH. God above... no.

ANNIE. You have to.

> ELISABETH *screams in frustration and storms out*. ANNIE *pours herself a shot of rum and downs it.*
>
> *Silence.*

Who is Thomas Thistlewood?

CERYS. The devil.

ANNIE. This island's full of devils.

CERYS. Me never see a man enjoy punishing slaves as much as that the devil there.

ANNIE. Who him is?

CERYS. Manager on Taylor's estates.

ANNIE. How do you know, you worked on a Taylor estate?

CERYS. Your mistress loans us field captives out, one harvest they put me to work in his sugar mill, his mill that never stops turning. All day and all night it turns and turns. All day and all night cut cane has to be pushed and pushed through its rollers. My friend fell asleep pressing cane juice, well she closed her eyes, just for a second and her hand got trapped, crushed between the rollers.

ANNIE. The mill kept turning?

CERYS. It nah stop fi nothing.

ANNIE. They didn't help her?

CERYS. Sugar must be made. The mill kept turning pulling her whole arm in, Thistlewood just ordered the overseer to hack her arm off with an axe. Then he ordered them beat her for spoiling the cane juice with her blood. Hacked her arm off then beat her. Hacked her arm off. Then beat her.

ANNIE. I heard you.

CERYS. She bled out there on the floor. Dead.

ANNIE. And the mill kept turning.

CERYS. Yes.

Long beat.

So you've never heard of Derby's dose?

ANNIE *shakes her head.*

CERYS. You never heard of Derby's dose?

ANNIE. No.

CERYS. It's a punishment Thistlewood create.

ANNIE. What is it?

CERYS. So the story goes, they say one very hot day in a very tough harvest, a captive named Derby was caught sucking juice out of a small stalk of sugar cane. Derby was whipped within an inch of his life but Thistlewood wasn't satisfied, he wasn't done. So he called on some of the other captives to hold Derby down, they did and then Thistlewood told his most loyal slave Egypt to shit in the boy's mouth –

ANNIE. You lie!

CERYS. Egypt did as he was ordered, then they put a gag on Derby's mouth and made him sit still in the sun with his mouth full for hours. He named the punishment after that poor man but anyone can get it for the smallest thing. Chopping cane too slow, eating food too fast. Talking too quiet, laughing too loud. I can't believe you never heard of Derby's dose.

ANNIE. ...What kind of wickedness?

CERYS. Boy, you really are protected up in here.

ANNIE. See. You see why I won't give this up? I am protected and while there is breath left in me I will fight with everything I have to keep this small bit of safety and peace I have found for myself.

CERYS. A captive on Taylor's estate is one of the leaders of our rebel –

ANNIE. I told you, don't bring up that fuckery again. This is the safest place for you to be –

50   THE WOMEN OF LLANRUMNEY

CERYS. I don't want safety, I want freedom.

ANNIE. Don't throw this away. Miss Elisabeth is no angel but none of them devilish evil things like Derby's dose go on up here inside the Great House of Llanrumney.

CERYS. How can you feel peace living in a world like this?

ANNIE. Easy, block all that out my mind, that's how. Don't look pon it, don't think pon it.

CERYS. How can I forget all –

ANNIE. Easy.

CERYS. I can't block out the pain of my people and pretend like they don't exist.

ANNIE. You have to.

CERYS. I won't.

ANNIE. You have to.

CERYS. I can't.

ANNIE. Don't look pon them, don't think pon them. Them that your friends, them that you love. All of them, block them out.

CERYS. Like you blocked me out?

ANNIE. Yes.

CERYS. Dumped me with old Miss Dilys.

ANNIE. And never looked back, I had to. For my peace, I had to. Didn't look at you, didn't hold you, just told her to take you. The master –

CERYS. Your father.

ANNIE. He'd threatened many times to auction you off and I didn't want to feel that pain. I wouldn't allow myself to love you, I didn't want to feel that heartbreak. You've heard the screams from a mother whose pickney gets sold away?

CERYS *nods*.

That agonising howl?

ACT THREE, SCENE TWO   51

CERYS. I've heard it, plenty times.

ANNIE. I protected myself from that pain. I'd had enough heartbreak in my life and I refused to feel any more. I numbed my heart to everything and everyone and my life got better... easier. People think it's easy for the slaves up in the big house, nice clothes, good food, soft bed. It's not, we're captives too. It wasn't easy like it is now, it hasn't always been like this for me. My father was a tyrant. A brutal man. Suffocating, possessive, lecherous man. It didn't take me long to understand why my mother tried to poison his food. I totally understand why she wanted to see him die a slow and painful death. But. I didn't want to meet an end like hers so I kept sweet. Didn't cuss, didn't struggle. Kept sweet. Until I met your father.

CERYS. My father? Who was he?

ANNIE. The love of my life, that's who he was.

CERYS. What was his name?

ANNIE. Samson.

CERYS. Tell me about him, I need to know.

ANNIE. He was born on a plantation in Saint Catherine's and sold to Llanrumney as a young man. He cost the master a lot of money as he was a very highly skilled gardener, he could name every tree, flower, plant. I'd watch him in the garden and he'd watch me in the cook house. He'd send me a flower every day. One very very happy year we had.

CERYS. Just one?

ANNIE. When I found out I was pregnant, your father decided to plan our escape, another foolish, stupid, dangerous plan. He wanted us to run away into the Blue Mountains and live with the Maroons in Moore Town. He didn't know about the treaty that had just been signed, he refused to believe me when I told him the Maroons had made a peace deal with the British. Just wouldn't believe it. That them same Maroons who had fought so long and so hard for the freedom they enjoyed had agreed to work with their old enslavers to hunt, capture and return any future runaways. He refused to believe it and he kept plotting. I refused to entertain his nonsense and our arguments caught the attention of Arthur, the master's valet. The master's eyes and ears. Arthur reported everything back to the master, the plot, the baby... you. And that was that.

CERYS. What happened?

ANNIE *shakes her head.*

ANNIE. That was that. Arthur was a bastard. Didn't give a fuck about anything or anyone, just himself and his position as head slave. A stone cold, heartless man. A monster. Unmoved by every brutality and indignity, didn't flinch, didn't cry, didn't care. He made himself indispensable to the master, was always by his side. Laughed with him, reasoned with him, advised him. If you didn't know any better you'd think he was a white man. Eventually, when the master was close to death, he freed Arthur and gave him his manumission papers. When Miss Elisabeth arrived, I made it my mission to become her Arthur. And I did, I became just like him stone cold and heartless. I didn't care about anybody but myself, I backstabbed and betrayed my way to the this position. I walked through hell to get to where I stand today. I earned this peace.

Scene Three

The next morning.

ANNIE *and* CERYS *are serving breakfast.* ELISABETH *and* TOMMY FLYNN *sit at the table.* ELISABETH *is clearly in pain, she sits silent and still as* TOMMY FLYNN *is scoffing down a load of food.*

ACT THREE, SCENE THREE

TOMMY FLYNN. To think I spent my boyhood out there with the niggers and now I'm sat here with you. A poor rednecked, red-leg out there holing cane and now I'm sat here with you. You know one thing I can't forget, no matter how hard I try. The smell. The stink of shit. Carrying baskets of stinking manure to fertilise the cane, I hated that job. Day in, day out, hauling tons of steaming animal shit in the burning sun. I fucking hated that job. I'd carry the basket on my head, easier that way, the niggers taught me that. It would stick in my hair, the shit, it would drip down my face. That fucking stink. That smell of shit, it haunts me. No matter how many fancy colognes I buy and douse myself in, I can still smell it, it's stuck to me.

TOMMY FLYNN stands, grabs a handful of food and stuffs them in his mouth as he makes his way to the door.

ELISABETH. Mr Flynn.

TOMMY FLYNN. Yes?

ELISABETH. Where are you going?

TOMMY FLYNN. I've business needs attending to, I should have left an hour ago.

ELISABETH. You're forgetting something.

TOMMY FLYNN. I am?

ELISABETH. Don't tease me.

TOMMY FLYNN. What?

ELISABETH. Please.

TOMMY FLYNN. What am I forgetting, Elisabeth?

ELISABETH. My money.

TOMMY FLYNN goes to leave.

Mr Flynn! I need that money –

TOMMY FLYNN. You'll be getting no money from me.

ELISABETH. You said –

TOMMY FLYNN. I won't be paying –

ELISABETH. Last night –

TOMMY FLYNN. I won't be paying for that shit, I've had more fun in church.

ELISABETH. We had an arrangement.

TOMMY FLYNN. Since when do arrangements mean anything to you? We had an arrangement before, remember, you reneged on it. Remember?

ELISABETH. No.

TOMMY FLYNN. Of course you don't. Let me remind you. I was an eleven-year-old orphan when I came to Llanrumney. My dear uncle had paid for my passage, gave me all the money he had in the world so I could make something of myself in the New World. My passage had been paid in full so that means my servitude contract, our arrangement, should have been four years. But you changed the terms of that contract, our arrangement, said four years wasn't long enough to cover the cost of my housing, food and clothing. Thats what you said and you added three more years. I tried to run away but you had me caught and flogged. Threatened to brand my face with the mark of a runaway. You should have let me go then, things would be very different for you now. I hated you. I hated that you owned me –

ELISABETH. But last night –

TOMMY FLYNN. Last night, I owned you.

TOMMY FLYNN winks and exits laughing. Silence.

ELISABETH. Fuck.

ELISABETH screams, smashing a plate on the table.

Fuck!!

ELISABETH paces angrily, picking up a bottle of rum pours herself a large glass.

ANNIE. Miss –

ACT THREE, SCENE THREE 55

ELISABETH. Shut up!

ANNIE. All is not –

ELISABETH. Fuck off, Annie!!

ELISABETH *downs the rum.*

ANNIE. All is not lost.

ELISABETH. Shut the fuck up. I don't want to hear anything from your mouth, I'll be taking no more stupid advice from you. I listened to you, you fucking moron, and now look at me... sullied! I've tainted myself for nothing. Last night....

ELISABETH *closes her eyes and shudders at the memory.* ANNIE *pours* ELISABETH *another shot of rum and hands it to her.*

I listened to you. I closed my eyes. Forced my mind elsewhere, but...

ELISABETH *shudders at the memory as she downs the rum.*

His breath... his sweat. I should have known that... I could see that... he got a great deal of pleasure from hurting and humiliating me. I should have know. Battered and bruised, for nothing.

ANNIE *is completely unmoved.*

ANNIE. Send for Mr Ainsworth.

ELISABETH. Don't you care? You're not listening to me.

ANNIE. Send for Mr Ainsworth, write to him and tell him you'll marry him.

ELISABETH. No.

ANNIE. You have –

ELISABETH. I will not –

ANNIE. You have no –

ELISABETH. I will not marry that man.

ANNIE. There is no other option, you have no other choice.

ELISABETH. I don't care, I will not marry that repugnant old toad.

ANNIE. You don't care?

Beat.

You don't care that Llanrumney will be lost. You don't care that this legacy, this Morgan family heritage entrusted to your safekeeping will be lost?

ELISABETH. If I marry Ainsworth, Llanrumney will still be lost. Me and everything I own, will belong to him.

ANNIE. That man is old, he'll die soon enough and then Llanrumney will be yours again.

ELISABETH. He has an army of sons. Llanrumney will be theirs, when he dies he'll leave everything that was once mine to his sons and I will be left at their mercy.

Trapped on this island in a loveless marriage, no autonomy, no freedom. I can't –

ANNIE. Behind close doors, maybe. But no one outside these walls will know. Marry Ainsworth and you'll save face. To Emily Evans and the rest of the parish, you will still be Lady of Llanrumney and a few other estates now too.

ELISABETH *thinks on this.*

The richest lady in Saint Mary.

ELISABETH. He has plantations in Saint George too.

ANNIE. The richest lady in Saint Mary and Saint George, can Emily Evans say that?

ANNIE *fetches the paper and pen.*

Write to him.

ANNIE *pulls out the chair.* ELISABETH *sits.*

Write him a love letter –

ELISABETH. A love letter?

ANNIE. Full of kind, loving words –

ELISABETH. Annie, no. I can't.

ANNIE. Overcompensate for past slights and apologise for your behaviour at Pemberton.

> ELISABETH *groans in frustration and begins to write.*

Blame it on the wine.

> ELISABETH *continues to write.*

Say that you have seen the error of your ways, that you regret declining his proposal and ask for him to attend you, urgently, but ask nice, lovingly.

> ELISABETH *writes.* ANNIE *watches over her shoulder.* ELISABETH *stops writing and passes the letter to* ANNIE.

> ANNIE *takes the letter and exits with it.* ELISABETH *picks up the bottle of rum and drinks straight from the bottle.*

Scene Four

The dining room. ELISABETH *is sat down, she is drunk.* CERYS *is stood by her, still and silent.*

MR AINSWORTH *enters, followed by* ANNIE. *He stands still, staring at* ELISABETH *waiting for her to speak.* ELISABETH *stares back.* ANNIE *signals to* ELISABETH *to stand.* ELISABETH *stands up, drunk and unsteady on her feet.*

ELISABETH. Hello.

> ANNIE *nods at* ELISABETH *encouraging her to speak.*

My love. Hello. My love.

> MR AINSWORTH *puts his hand to his heart, touched by her words.*

MR AINSWORTH. I've waited so long to hear you call me that. Do you know how long I've ached to hear you call me that?

ELISABETH *hesitates not knowing what to say.*

I received your letter. I set out for Llanrumney as soon as I read it.

Silence.

I was shocked to read of your change of heart. What brought that on?

ELISABETH *is trying to stay steady on her feet and look sober.*

ELISABETH. My darling Edmund. Dearest. Since our last meeting... I have thought of nothing else but you. My darling. Sweet darling.

MR AINSWORTH. Why, sweet Lizzie, why?

ELISABETH. Why?

MR AINSWORTH *nods. Silence.*

Why?

MR AINSWORTH. Why? Because at our last encounter, our last few encounters, you were really quite rude, brash and nasty to be frank. Why? What has melted your ice-cold heart?

ELISABETH. Ice cold –

MR AINSWORTH. Yes. Ice cold.

Beat.

ELISABETH. Because. I realise now....

Unseen by MR AINSWORTH, ANNIE *mouths 'I was a fool' to* ELISABETH.

I was a fool. I was a fool to run from your love. I ran from your love because... I was scared. But I am not scared any more, I know now I love you.

MR AINSWORTH *is touched by this. He takes a moment to compose himself. Beat.*

MR AINSWORTH. Why?

ELISABETH. Why do I love you?

MR AINSWORTH. Yes. Why, all of a sudden? When I have, for years, tried in vain to court you, woo you. I have tried, in vain, for years, to make you love me.

Why now do you all of a sudden no longer feel the need to mock and ostracise me? Why now all of a sudden do you love me, Elisabeth? Answer me honestly.

Beat.

ELISABETH. Your handsome face. Your handsome face has consumed my every thought and I realise now that I was wrong. And yes, I do want to marry you.

MR AINSWORTH. For many years, my sweet Lizzy, I have held a very dear place for you in my heart.

ELISABETH. I know.

MR AINSWORTH. I have tried to make you happy. I have supported you, protected you –

ELISABETH. I know.

MR AINSWORTH. I have loaned you money, copious amounts of money. I have paid of your shopping debts, your gambling debts. Defended you against malicious gossip and salacious hearsay –

ELISABETH. What?

MR AINSWORTH. But I –

ELISABETH. What gossip?

MR AINSWORTH. I can not, will not, continue to let you make a fool of me. You play with my heart for sport it seems.

ELISABETH. No.

MR AINSWORTH. Yes.

ELISABETH. My dear –

MR AINSWORTH. You must take me for an absolute fool.

ELISABETH. No.

MR AINSWORTH. Yes! I asked you to answer me honestly. When I asked you why you had a change of heart, I needed you to answer me honestly.

ELISABETH. I did –

MR AINSWORTH. You did not. You have run out of options, that is the honest answer.

ELISABETH. What... no.

MR AINSWORTH. Run out of money, run out of favour, run out of options.

Beat.

Saint Mary is awash with chatter about your predicament, your debt, your desperation. You've destroyed this estate, sullied yourself and ruined your good name. Am I that repulsive, that abhorrent that you would whore yourself to an Irish serf before me?

ELISABETH. That bastard Flynn!

MR AINSWORTH. You have shamed yourself! You will be shunned by all decent society, no invitations, no banquets, no balls. You are now and will forever be a pariah in this parish. Goodbye, sweet Lizzy, goodbye.

MR AINSWORTH *leaves. Silence.*

ELISABETH. That's it.

ANNIE. No.

ELISABETH. It's over.

ANNIE. No Miss Elisabeth, no.

ELISABETH. I am now and will forever be a pariah in this town, that's what he said. My time is Jamaica is done, I've lost everything.

ANNIE. We'll sell the Wedgwood. These, the green set, the cream set. All of it. Many things of worth you have, miss. We'll sell as much as we can to pay what you owe. The gold flatware. Many fine things you have. The porcelain. The lacquered furniture. The baroque dressing table, the only one on the island, that's what you said miss. The only one on the island?

ELISABETH. Yes, it is.

ANNIE. We'll sell it.

ELISABETH. It cost a fortune –

ANNIE. Then it'll fetch a good price! The paintings.

ELISABETH. Annie, I could sell every piece of furniture I own and I'd still be in debt.

ANNIE. The Venetian glass?

ELISABETH *drinks*.

ELISABETH. Dumb nigger.

Beat.

ANNIE. Miss?

ELISABETH. I blame you –

ANNIE. Now, miss, it wasn't me who –

ELISABETH. Cut me off one more time, I dare you. Speak out of turn one more time, I dare you!

ANNIE *says nothing*.

I'm selling Llanrumney. I'm selling Llanrumney and every thing in it, every pot, every pan, dinner service, hog, horse and nigger.

Silence.

And I will return back to Monmouthshire and start again. If you behave and watch your mouth, I might take you with me. Maybe.

ELISABETH *looks directly at* CERYS (*this must be the first time in the play that* ELISABETH *acknowledges* CERYS's *presence*).

ANNIE. My daughter, miss.

ELISABETH. You don't have a daughter, Annie.

ANNIE. Yes, Miss Elisabeth, I do.

ELISABETH. No you don't. What's your name, girl?

CERYS *does not answer.*

ANNIE. Her name is Cerys, miss.

ELISABETH *laughs.*

ELISABETH. Anwen and Cerys. My cousin had a great sense of humour giving every negro he owned a Welsh name. Though it's much better than naming them after pharaohs like they do at Haywood Hall. I was served dinner by a Rameses once.

ELISABETH *walks over to* CERYS *and studies her.*

Way too dark to be a lady's maid. Not that it matters now.

ELISABETH *inspects* CERYS, *squeezing her arm and thigh.*

Belongs in the field.

ELISABETH *touches* CERYS's *baby bump and smiles.*

That'll fetch me a decent amount.

ELISABETH *exits.*

ANNIE. We need to polish the silverware. Then prepare for dinner. Fetch the clean bedding from the laundry, then pick some lemongrass and lavender for her bath.

Silence. ANNIE *busies herself with chores.*

CERYS. You were blessed to get that year, that one happy year. Truly blessed. To experience all'a them things that make a life worth living. Rebellions aren't just fought in battle y'know, they happen every time we connect and love each other. Love is a revolutionary act, can't nobody

tell me different. Despite them telling us we can't, we will
connect and love each other anyway. Mother, child, friend,
lover. Despite them telling us we can't we will laugh and
we will sing, we will dance to the drums they try to ban.
Despite them, no matter the time that's passed or the distance
between us, we will love each other. Y'hear?

ANNIE *nods.*

They take our names, our languages, our culture but they can
not take our love for each other, that is something they can't
touch or destroy. Understand?

ANNIE *nods.* CERYS *hugs* ANNIE *tight.*

Scene Five

The next day.

SIMON TAYLOR *and* ELISABETH *are sat at the dining table,
lots of paperwork is strewn across the table. On the floor around*
SIMON TAYLOR*'s feet are iron wrist shackles and an iron gag.*

ANNIE *and* CERYS *are serving them tea.*

SIMON TAYLOR.…and, the eighty-nine male slaves were
valued at three thousand pounds, for the ninety-eight women,
seven thousand and five hundred pounds. One indentured
servant at forty pounds. We valued the twenty-three boys
at eight hundred and five pounds and the thirteen girls at
nine hundred and twenty. The total value of all the slaves at
Llanrumney is twelve thousand, two hundred and sixty-five
pounds.

SIMON TAYLOR *passes* ELISABETH *a piece of paper to
sign, she signs it.*

For the other livestock, such as cattle –

ELISABETH. No more tea, Annie, for the love of God no more
tea.

ANNIE *picks up the rum and starts pouring.*

SIMON TAYLOR. And for the other livestock such as cattle, one hundred pounds.

SIMON TAYLOR *passes a piece of paper to* ELISABETH. ELISABETH *signs the paper and hands it back to him.* SIMON TAYLOR *stands up and begins to tidy up and gather his papers.*

And that, Miss Morgan, concludes our business.

ELISABETH. Thank you, Mr Taylor.

SIMON TAYLOR. I wish you a safe voyage back home.

ELISABETH. I'm dreading it. I swore never in my life would I do that journey again.

SIMON TAYLOR. It's a killer.

ELISABETH. Yes, it killed my brother and it nearly killed me.

SIMON TAYLOR. Well you can travel back in a much more comfortable class this time.

SIMON TAYLOR *gathers his things, picking up the iron shackles.*

ELISABETH. Yes, I can, that something I suppose.

SIMON TAYLOR. I will transfer all of Llanrumney's field hands to my other estates and move a select group of skilled slaves here to tend to the fungal problem.

ELISABETH. Yes, of course, that's fine –

SIMON TAYLOR *grabs* CERYS*'s arms.*

It's your property now.

SIMON TAYLOR *pulls* CERYS*'s arms behind her back, locking her hands in the shackles.*

CERYS (*to* ANNIE). Ye nye nkowa bio.

SIMON TAYLOR *slaps* CERYS *around the head.*

SIMON TAYLOR. Shut up. English only.

ELISABETH *hands* SIMON TAYLOR *the iron gag*.

CERYS. When the sky is dark, remember, ye nye nkowa bio.

SIMON TAYLOR *fastens the iron gag around* CERYS *mouth, silencing her.*

SIMON TAYLOR. Shut. Up.

CERYS *is gagged and bound*.

As discussed, I will let the lady's maid stay with you and help you prepare for your journey home. My bookkeeper Thistlewood will fetch her before you depart.

ELISABETH. That's very kind, thank you.

SIMON TAYLOR *pulls* CERYS *towards the door.*

SIMON TAYLOR. God bless you, Miss Morgan, may Christ guide, protect and grant you a safe calm passage.

ELISABETH. God bless you too, Mr Taylor. Goodbye.

SIMON TAYLOR *and* CERYS *exit*. ELISABETH *turns to* ANNIE.

I'll rest on the veranda until dinner. Tell cook I want to approve the menu for second breakfast tomorrow, Emily Evans will be joining me and I want our last meal together to be one she'll never forget.

ANNIE *does not reply*.

Annie.

ANNIE *does not reply*.

Annie. What you are unable to understand is that I owe a huge amount of money to a lot of people. To pay what I owe in full I had to sell everything, every asset I had, including you. You don't understand, you've never had to pay a bill in your life, you could never understand what I am going through.

ANNIE *says nothing*.

Annie. Housekeepers are of high value and as you are a housekeeper with decades of experience, you were one of my most valuable assets.

Silence.

Not that I owe you any kind of explanation.

Silence.

No lemongrass in my bath tonight, just lavender.

ELISABETH *exits.*

ACT FOUR

Two days later.

Night-time. The sky is dark.

ANNIE *is packing clothes into a large oak trunk.* ELISABETH *dressed in a nightgown, she sits drinking at the table.*

ELISABETH. I wonder what they'll all think when they see me again?

Silence as ANNIE *continues to pack.*

It's been twenty years, I wonder what they'll say?

Silence as ANNIE *continues to pack.*

If my aunt is anything like she was before I left, it won't be anything nice. Though she'll say it in a sweet tone with a condescending smile, she'd always say the most hurtful things with a smile. I wonder if they'll even recognise me, do you think they'll recognise me?

ANNIE *doesn't reply*

Twenty years is an awfully long time, have I aged?

ANNIE *doesn't reply.*

Have. I. Aged?

ANNIE. Yes.

ELISABETH. Have I aged badly? That's what I am asking Annie, have I aged badly? Has the sun made my skin shrivel up like an old satsuma?

ANNIE. Yes.

ELISABETH. How dare you.

ANNIE. Everybody ages, everybody changes.

ELISABETH. I wasted my best years on this barbaric island. I have changed, my being has been irrevocably changed by this godforsaken place. That naive sweet young thing who sailed off for the New World with nothing but a dream, died within me the second she arrived in Kingston. You don't understand, you could never understand because you were born into all of this, you're used to it. But this island made a monster out of me, something died inside me when I stepped foot in this hell. The heat knocked me off my feet, it suffocated me and the smell choked me, that asphyxiating stench of Kingston Harbour. Piss, shit and rotting flesh, that's the smell, the stench of death that whiffs from the galley of all those slave ships.

Changed me. I've arrived in hell, that's what I thought to myself as I walked past the slave auctions. Petrified of every sight and sound. You didn't blink an eye, I'll never forget that, you didn't flinch but I was terrified, traumatised by it all.

Hundreds of black brutish beast like bodies, everywhere. Surrounded. This must be hell, I thought to myself, it has to be.

ANNIE. You stayed.

ELISABETH. What?

ANNIE. In hell. You happily made a life here, in hell.

Beat.

ELISABETH. Are you insinuating that I'm the devil?

ANNIE. You could have gone home.

ELISABETH. Watch your tone, Annie.

ANNIE. You could have gone home, miss.

ELISABETH. How? I was sick with that same deadly fever that killed my darling brother, don't you remember? Burning up, my eyes were yellow, my skin was yellow. I was dying, Annie, you really don't remember that?

ANNIE. Of course I remember –

ELISABETH. I was at death's door.

ANNIE. I remember, I saved your life. I nursed you through the relentless headache, raging fever and delirium, nursed you through the nausea, the bloodied black vomit. Comforted you, calmed you, held you. Nursed you back from the brink of death with every bush remedy and tincture I knew. I saved your life and then I taught you how to survive this barbaric island.

ELISABETH. I didn't ask you to.

ANNIE. I never did that for her, I did more for you than I ever did for my own child.

ELISABETH. And that's my fault?

ANNIE does not reply.

I forced you to abandon the child I didn't know existed? That's my fault?

ELISABETH *laughs*.

You're pathetic. You never once, in all these years, spoke of being a mother.

ANNIE. Because –

ELISABETH. Because you are a selfish cold-hearted, ruthless woman. Who only ever cared about protecting yourself, your position and your privileges.

ANNIE. Yes –

ELISABETH. Aren't you?

ANNIE. I was, yes.

ELISABETH. You say I clung to you, we both know that's not true. You clung to me, wouldn't let any other house slave near me. I actually never officially appointed you housekeeper, you assumed the role. You appointed yourself. You made yourself indispensable, spying on your fellow negroes, subjugating, denigrating them all to curry favour and secure your position. You made yourself indispensable, *you* clung to me.

ANNIE. Because I wanted to be free. That's why I clung to you. I wanted you to see me, talk with me, laugh with me, look me in my eyes and see me, Annie. Not a slave, not some object at your service. I wanted you to see me every day as a human being worthy of freedom.

ELISABETH. Freedom?

ELISABETH *laughs*.

ANNIE. I lived my whole life desperate for the peace I thought manumission would bring me.

The blast of a conch-shell horn sounds out loudly.
ELISABETH *bolts up panicked*. ANNIE *does not move*.

ELISABETH. Did you hear that?

ANNIE. But no peace can come to a land like this.

ELISABETH. Annie, did you hear that?

ANNIE. No peace can come to a land where such brutality and wickedness –

The blast of the conch-shell horn sounds loudly again.

ELISABETH. Annie!

ANNIE. This system –

ELISABETH. That sound –

ANNIE. Slavery –

ELISABETH. The horn, that's the sound of –

ANNIE. War.

ELISABETH. Rebellion!

ANNIE. Yes.

ELISABETH *panics*, ANNIE *does not move*.

ELISABETH. Go and find out what's happening!

ANNIE. Rebellion, that is what is happening.

The blast of the conch shell sounds out loudly.

Can't nobody out there tell us what we don't already know.

Sounds of doors slamming, floor boards creaking, heavy footsteps rushing about.

ELISABETH. Oh God, not again, please God not again.

ANNIE *goes to the window to look out.*

ANNIE. No peace can come to a land like this.

ELISABETH. Annie, come away from there.

ANNIE *does not move.*

ANNIE. Again and again the wars won't stop because no peace can come until slavery ends.

ELISABETH. Annie, come away from the window! If they see us, they'll kill us.

ANNIE. Us?

ELISABETH. Yes us, me and you. Us.

The sound of distant drumming can be heard.

We have to get out of here, we have to get to Kingston.

ELISABETH *grabs some clothes from the trunk and shoves them into* ANNIE's *hands.*

Help me dress.

ELISABETH *removes her nightgown.* ANNIE *does not move.*

Then find the overseer or someone, anyone, who can drive me in the carriage to safety.

ANNIE. You?

ELISABETH. Us!

ELISABETH *has undressed and is stood in her undergarments, arms stretched waiting to be dressed by* ANNIE.

The drumming intensifies and the chants of 'Ye nye nkowa bio' begins.

Annie, come on!!

ANNIE. You can't dress yourself?

ELISABETH.... of course –

ANNIE *throws the clothes at* ELISABETH.

ANNIE. Then do it.

ELISABETH *picks up the clothes and begins to dress herself, she is not used to doing this and struggles.*

ELISABETH. Please help me. They'll kill me. Please.

The sound of the drumming and chanting draws closer.

I am sorry. I'm sorry if I have been a cruel mistress to you. I told you, this island made a monster out of me!

ANNIE. You were a monster when you arrived. You sailed across the oceans with dreams of becoming rich off human bondage. You were a monster when you arrived.

ELISABETH. I'm sorry. Help me please, I'm sorry. I will write to Simon Taylor. I promise. I will write to Taylor and insist on keeping you.

The sound of the chanting and drumming surrounds them.

I will insist on keeping you and I will buy you back. I promise!

The sound of the violent rebellion surrounds them, e.g. screams, things being smashed, gunshots.

I will buy you back and then I will free you, Annie. Please just help me get out of here.

The dark sky is now filled with the colours of fire.

ACT FOUR 73

ELISABETH *rushes to the door to leave.*

Annie, come on! I promise. I swear on all that is holy, I will get you your manumission papers, you will be free.

ANNIE. Real freedom can't be written on a piece of paper, that's not real freedom. Real freedom is taken, demanded by all for the benefit of all.

ELISABETH *rushes out of the room in fear and panic. The sounds of the rebellion intensifies.* ANNIE *is left alone, she mouths along with the chanting.*

Ye nye nkowa bio.

The sound of ELISABETH*'s screams ring out.*

Ye nye nkowa bio.

Lights down.

A Nick Hern Book

The Women of Llanrumney first published in Great Britain as a paperback original in 2024 by Nick Hern Books Limited, The Glasshouse, 49a Goldhawk Road, London W12 8QP, in association with Sherman Theatre, Cardiff.

The Women of Llanrumney copyright © 2024 Azuka Oforka

Azuka Oforka has asserted her right to be identified as the author of this adaptation

Cover image by Ana Pinto and Burning Red

Designed and typeset by Nick Hern Books, London
Printed in Great Britain by Mimeo Ltd, Huntingdon, Cambridgeshire PE29 6XX

A CIP catalogue record for this book is available from the British Library

ISBN 978 1 83904 346 8

CAUTION All rights whatsoever in this play are strictly reserved. Requests to reproduce the text in whole or in part should be addressed to the publisher.

Amateur Performing Rights Applications for performance, including readings and excerpts, by amateurs in the English language should be addressed to the Performing Rights Manager, Nick Hern Books, The Glasshouse, 49a Goldhawk Road, London W12 8QP, *tel* +44 (0)20 8749 4953, *email* rights@nickhernbooks.co.uk, except as follows:

Australia: ORiGiN Theatrical, *tel* +61 (2) 8514 5201,
email enquiries@originmusic.com.au, *web* www.origintheatrical.com.au

New Zealand: Play Bureau, 20 Rua Street, Mangapapa, Gisborne 4010,
tel +64 21 258 3998, *email* info@playbureau.com

Professional Performing Rights Rights Applications for performance by professionals in any medium and in any language throughout the world should be addressed in the first instance to Nick Hern Books, see contact details above.

No performance of any kind may be given unless a licence has been obtained. Applications should be made before rehearsals begin. Publication of this play does not necessarily indicate its availability for amateur performance.

www.nickhernbooks.co.uk/environmental-policy

www.nickhernbooks.co.uk

facebook.com/nickhernbooks

twitter.com/nickhernbooks